WERE
YOU?

DISCARD

D1157920

BOOKS BY GLORIA CHADWICK

Discovering Your Past Lives

Spirituality and Self-Empowerment

Somewhere Over the Rainbow: A Soul's Journey Home

Reincarnation and Your Past-Life Memories

Parallel Lives: A Mystical Journey

Soul Shimmers: Awakening Your Spiritual Self

Magical Mind, Magical Life

The Key to Self-Empowerment

Happy Ways to Heal the Earth

Life Is Just a Dream

Exploring Your Past Lives: A Workbook

Psychic Senses: How to Develop Your Innate Powers

Inner Journeys: Meditations and Visualizations

Future Lives: Discovering & Understanding Your Destiny

The Path to Publishing Your Book

The Write Way

Recipe for a Cookbook

Foods & Flavors of San Antonio

The Path to Self-Publishing

Change Your Mind, Change Your Life

Zen Coffee: A Guide to Mindful Meditation

WHO WERE YOU?

A DO-IT-YOURSELF GUIDE TO PAST LIFE REGRESSION

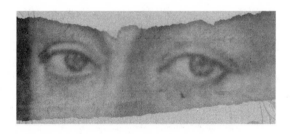

Gloria Chadwick

STERLING

New York / London
www.sterlingpublishing.com

To learn more about the author, visit www.chadwickpages.com
and www.mysticalmindscapes.com.

STERLING and the distinctive Sterling logo are registered trademarks of
Sterling Publishing Co., Inc.

Library of Congress Cataloging-in-Publication Data Available

10 9 8 7 6 5 4 3 2 1

Published by Sterling Publishing Co., Inc.
387 Park Avenue South, New York, NY 10016
© 2009 by Gloria Chadwick
Distributed in Canada by Sterling Publishing
C/o Canadian Manda Group, 165 Dufferin Street
Toronto, Ontario, Canada M6K 3H6
Distributed in the United Kingdom by GMC Distribution Services
Castle Place, 166 High Street, Lewes, East Sussex, England BN7 1XU
Distributed in Australia by Capricorn Link (Australia) Pty. Ltd.
P.O. Box 704, Windsor, NSW 2756, Australia

Sterling ISBN 978-1-4027-6003-7

For information about custom editions, special sales, premium and
corporate purchases, please contact Sterling Special Sales
Department at 800-805-5489 or specialsales@sterlingpublishing.com.

This book is

dedicated to the philosopher.

Thanks for sharing your knowledge

and for journeying with me on the rainbow path.

CONTENTS

PART II—VIBRATIONS

Relaxation is the art of quieting your conscious mind, relaxing your physical body, and opening up your subconscious mind. Being in a meditative frame of mind. Soothing suggestions to relax your body, and to open up and enhance your subconscious awareness. *Sidetracks . . . Present Purposes:* Shows how relaxation can be used every day for minimizing and eliminating stress, tension, worries, and negativity while offering you a wonderful way to refresh and replenish yourself in body, mind, and spirit. *Side Trip . . . Healing and Harmonizing Your Body, Mind, and Spirit.*

Resonating with rainbow colors inside your soul. Feeling and experiencing how the energy vibrations of the colors in the rainbow affect your subconscious awareness and influence your seven spiritual energy bodies. Colors can hold past life trauma. How to release the trauma through the vibrations of the color. *Sidetracks . . . Present and Past Life Purposes:* Discusses the endocrine system and chakras that are associated with each color. Feeling and focusing on the energies of the colors. Ways to use the energies and vibrations of rainbow colors for many positive purposes on both physical and spiritual levels. *Side Trip . . . The Rainbow Path:* Finding gifts in the spiritual vibrations of the rainbow.

Explains what the universal energies of white light are, how to attune yourself with the vibrations, and the many ways it can be used during your past life journey. Shows the primary purposes of white light—for spiritual protection and healing during the regression. Recognizing and remembering what the light is—the natural vibration of your soul. *Sidetracks . . . Good Vibrations:* Describes the many benefits of white light and the physical, mental, emotional, and spiritual ways you can use it in every part of your life.

A spiritual sanctuary is a place of harmony within your heart, mind, and soul where you're completely in tune with your spiritual vibrations, where your soul can renew and refresh itself, and where you can rest and reflect. Getting in touch with yourself and being in tune with the peaceful vibrations of your inner nature. Ways to use this sacred space before, during, and after your past life regression. *Sidetracks . . . Present Purposes:* Ways to use your sanctuary in your everyday life.

Tuning in to your true spiritual nature and turning on your spiritual awareness. Remembering your higher self—the most spiritual, knowledgeable part of you. The various roles your higher self plays in your life. Why your higher self appears as an angel from time to time, and how he or she is the highest aspect of your soul, the immortal flame of your existence. Reuniting and becoming reacquainted with your higher self, who will be your mentor and inner guide into and through your past life memories. Understanding your guide's purpose during your past life regression. Looking and listening within. Trusting your inner knowing. *Sidetracks . . . Present Purposes:* Provides information about the spiritual side of yourself and how your inner guide plays a vital role in every part of your life. How to blend your physical energies with your higher self to bring your higher self awareness into all your everyday experiences.

Friends, lovers, enemies, and special family members are souls you've known before. Becoming aware of people from the past who are also in the present. How to recognize and remember them. The roles they played then and the roles they play now. Past/present relationships. Soul mates and kindred spirits. How the energies of emotions continue through time. *Side Trip . . . Resolving Relationships:* Becoming aware of past life connections, then resolving present relationship problems with people who were in your past lives. *Sidetracks . . . Present Purposes:* Healing your present relationships. *Side Trips . . . A Love Meditation for Your Heart and Soul, and Meeting Your Soulmate; Drawing Him or Her to You.*

What karma is and what it means to you. How and why past life events show up in the present. The reasons for and purposes of karma. The nature of karma. Cause and effect. Good karma/bad karma. Free will. Continuations and carryovers. How the past can come back to either help you or haunt you in the present. How to change the energies of past life experiences, how your choices and feelings will affect and alter the present, and how they will modify your future. Coming full circle. Better balancing. How to heal karma, and any soul pain or trauma, from past life events. Ways to bless and let go of situations, emotions, and other souls— to release and heal them in loving ways. The process of positive change. A four-step plan to balance your karma. *Sidetracks . . . Present Purposes:* Explains the benefits of balancing in the context of creating positive experiences in your current life. How healing the present heals the past.

Finding and fulfilling the purpose that you chose to accomplish in this lifetime. Becoming aware of past life purposes and how they relate to and influence your present purpose. Knowing what's inside your soul. Traveling the path that's right for you. *Side Trip . . . Following the Path to Your Purpose.*

What mind-tripping is and how to do it. The power of your mind to take you places and show you things. Traveling on the energies of your soul. Imagination and made-up memories. Daydreams and reveries. Various methods of mind-tripping. *Side Trips . . . Roundabout Reveries:* Play with who you were before and what you've done. Go with the flow of karma to take you into a past life. *Side Trips . . . Tripping Through Time:* Practice trips to help you get the feel of a past life regression and get into the flow of time.

How the past blends into the present to create a sense of timelessness. Past and present energies; the way they weave through time. How to relate interconnected past experiences with your present experiences to understand how they interact with and influence each other. What you need to know, both before and along the way, as you journey into and through your past life memories. Shows the ins and outs, and several perspectives and perceptions of viewing events in your past lives. *Sidetracks . . . Past and Present Life Purposes:* Offers various ways to use these perceptions and perspectives to gain an overall, expanded picture of your present life to view current experiences and situations, and to help you make clearer choices and decisions. Exploring your intuition and inner knowing within these perspectives. Reading scenes and situations in your present life. Mind-tripping into your present experiences to gain insight and resolution to present problems, whether they originated in a past life or were created in your present life. Shows how to avoid incurring present karma that will appear in the future.

Planning and preparing. Things to do and see during your past life journey. The beginning steps. Finding your focus to start your travels. Acclimating yourself into your past life. What to do if your mind goes blank or the images are fuzzy. Traveling through related lifetimes to become aware of interconnected events. Focusing on pivot points that allow you to turn in any direction. Understanding what you're seeing and feeling. Going with the flow. What to do inside your past life experiences. Getting unstuck. Giving yourself directions and prompts along the way. Listening to your higher self. How to handle past life pain and trauma. Going through the death scene. Immortality and eternity.

PART V—SOUL SHIMMERS   171

INTRODUCTION

Over the years since my first book on reincarnation—*Discovering Your Past Lives*—was published, I've received numerous letters from readers requesting referrals to help them find a hypnotist in their area who could do past life regressions or asking for more information about how to do a past life regression for themselves. I've written this book to make the complete process of past life regression easily accessible and available to all of you who want to know and learn more about your past lives, to remember and reexperience the events and emotions in them, and to understand how the past interconnects with and influences your present life.

This book is my way of sharing the knowledge I have acquired and is offered to help you remember and understand who you were before, how the events and emotions in your past lives have shaped and led you to who you are now, and how they will influence who you will become. It's a guide that offers you a complete do-it-yourself past life regression; the only things missing are the hypnotist and the recliner. These you supply yourself in the form of your higher self, who is your inner, very knowledgeable, and capable guide—much better than a hypnotist—and a comfortable, quiet place in your own home—much better for relaxing and being more comfortable than a hypnotist's office.

Helpful hints and comprehensive coverage of everything that is associated with a past life regression are in this book. The text gives thorough background information and directions that are necessary to know before, during, and after the regression. It tells you everything you need to know—and more—about traveling into and through your past lives so that you can do a complete past life regression for yourself by using self-hypnosis. Some of the information that is integral to a past life regression—including the rainbow relaxation, white light, spiritual sanctuary, and higher self—was included in my first book; it is offered in this book in a revised, updated form.

The text is interwoven with an in-depth script for getting into your subconscious mind and accessing your past life memories. The *italicized* script offers word-for-word, step-by-step instructions for your journey into and through the events and emotions in your past lives, and guides you through balancing your karma as well as healing past life events. The Appendix contains the complete script but eliminates some of the detailed, supporting information contained within each chapter that gives you a substantial background to build on.

Most of the chapters give an overview, describing how to use the information in the script, what other people have experienced, and what to expect while giving you a preview of things you'll most likely be encountering. Knowing what you're getting into and what to expect ahead of time alleviates any doubts and reinforces your desire to find out more about your past lives. Each chapter is a consecutive step in your past life journey.

Included are sidetracks that show you how you can use the same information in this book in your present life for many other positive purposes besides journeying into your past lives. There are also side trips that provide you with interesting adventures and enlightening excursions to experience along the way as you travel into your soul. Some side trips take you into parts of your past lives; others offer you soulful meditations. You might want to write down your reflections after each journey to help you further open up your past life memories.

The benefits of remembering your past lives are understanding how the events and emotions in your past lives relate to and influence your present life, then using that knowledge, insight, and awareness to help you in your present life. By reexperiencing what you experienced in the past, you become aware of your soul lessons, and you decide how to best balance your karma, which is cause and effect—the energies of events from past lives that surface in the present—to help you evolve your soul. This is basically what reincarnation is all about.

I've remembered many of my past lives, some in fragments and fleeting images, and others more vividly. The past life I remember very clearly and in the greatest detail relates most directly to who I am now and to what I do in this life—teaching, writing, and sharing my knowledge. That lifetime was the one I experienced in Egypt as a high priest–turned–philosopher. The story is told in my novel, *Somewhere Over the Rainbow: A Soul's Journey Home*.

As you open up your past life memories, you'll remember the events, emotions, and relationships in the lifetime or lifetimes that relate most directly to this lifetime, along with bits and pieces of other events in past lives that are relevant to what is occurring in your present life. This is because the energies and experiences of the past are in harmony with the choices you've made regarding what you want and need to experience in this lifetime. You'll understand how your past life affects what you're currently experiencing and why the influence is being felt in the present. By exploring your past lives, and understanding their effect on your present life, you'll find the answers and insights that give meaning and purpose to your life, and you'll understand the true nature of your soul.

Whenever you're ready, find a quiet place, a comfortable chair or couch, and begin your journey into your past lives.

PART I

PRELIMINARIES

———

1

BEGINNINGS

Before I begin a session with my clients, I ask them to fill out the following questionnaire. It helps me to better know how to guide them and what's important to them. Since you're doing this past life regression for yourself, it will help you become clearer on your reasons for wanting to know about the events and emotions contained within your past life memories. You might want to write down your answers to the following questions or you may prefer to think about them, to open up the information in your subconscious mind to help you prepare for one of the most exciting, informative, and enlightening journeys you'll ever experience.

SECTION I: REASONS FOR REQUESTING
A PAST LIFE REGRESSION

1. What is your specific reason for wanting a past life regression?

2. What knowledge or insight do you want to acquire through a past life regression?

3. Is there a question you'd like the answers to, or a problem or difficulty in your life right now that you'd like to solve through a past life regression? If yes, explain the question, problem, or difficulty. How do you feel your question or your present situation relates to a past life?

4. How do you feel a past life regression will help you in your present life?

Section II: Background Information

1. Have you experienced memories of a past life before? If yes, give details.

If you're already aware of past life memories, through spontaneous recall, intuition, or a sense about what happened or what might have happened, these may be expanded upon or enhanced in your regression. Many times events from past lives are reflected in similar present experiences and may surface through déjà vu or show themselves in your dreams. We'll cover more of this in Chapter Three.

2. Have you been regressed to a past life before? If yes, give details.

If you've already experienced a past life regression, the memories you've previously become aware of will very likely be further enhanced as you conduct your own past life regression, and you can approach the session already having a good idea of what to expect.

3. What is your personal belief about reincarnation?

Your beliefs about past lives will color the information you become aware of and the way you become aware of it. Knowing what your beliefs and feelings are about reincarnation will help you to understand the context in which your memories surface.

You don't necessarily have to believe in reincarnation as a prerequisite for your past life memories to surface. They'll surface, if the time is right and when the past/present energies align, whether you believe in past lives or not.

I once heard a joke at a hypnosis conference that went something like this: A client approaches a hypnotist for a past life regression. The hypnotist asks the client if she believes in reincarnation. The client replies that no, she does not. It's all a bunch of hooey, but she'd like to see what the hypnotist can do. The hypnotist replies that it's okay if she doesn't believe in reincarnation; she'll believe it in her next lifetime.

A hypnotist doesn't have any power to bring your past life memories to the surface. What the hypnotist has is a special skill in the wording of the suggestions given to you, and the manner in which the past life regression is conducted, that will help you open up your past life memories. You have that same skill within you and it can be easily learned. We'll cover this in the next chapter.

4. Have you had any spiritual experiences, such as an astral projection, a near-death experience, or being visited by someone who has passed on? If yes, give details.

If you've had these or similar experiences, then you're familiar with the frequencies of energy contained within these realms.

During your past life regression, you may travel into and through these same vibrations of energy. (The answer to this question helps me know where my clients are in terms of previous spiritual experiences and their response to them. It gives me a better idea of how to connect with my clients on a soul level and to best guide them during the regression.)

5. List any classes you've taken or books you've read relating to reincarnation and past lives. How have these classes or the information in the books helped you to open up your inner spiritual awareness and to become aware of past life memories?

If you've previously read about reincarnation or attended a past life workshop, you've already built the background and foundation for your spiritual awareness to surface regarding past lives, and you may have become aware of relationships and situations in previous lives. The things you've already studied and experienced will help you, and will likely affect and influence what you experience and the way you experience it in your past life regression.

(The answer to this question shows me where my clients are in terms of their spiritual awareness. By knowing what classes my clients have attended and what books they've read, it also clues me in as to how to phrase my words and suggestions in a context that my clients will be familiar and comfortable with, and will coincide with their belief system and previous experiences in exploring past lives.)

6. Are you familiar with and do you understand the following terms? *Karma. Higher self. White light protection.*

If you're familiar with these terms, you understand what they are and how they operate. They are integral in a past life regression because they are part and parcel of what occurs during a past life regression. These terms will be explained, in detail, in several chapters of this book.

7. Do you meditate or use a particular method for relaxing and entering a more aware level of mind?

If you already have a method or technique that you like and use, you may want to continue with it since you're familiar and comfortable with it, and you know you can reach the proper frame of mind with it. But try the progressive relaxation and rainbow method offered in this book to see which one will work most effectively for you in opening up your subconscious awareness and your past life memories.

REVIEWING YOUR ANSWERS

Let's look over your answers to the first section of this questionnaire. If you haven't answered the questions, please do so now. Don't use the following explanations as a cheat sheet. You'll only be cheating yourself.

The reasons for wanting a past life regression vary from individual to individual. A few people think it would fun to know about their past lives, but aren't seriously interested in truly knowing what occurred then. They only want the information so they can talk about it to their friends, and because it's a novelty. If this is your reason, I have bad news for you. You probably won't be able to access your past life memories because you don't have a specific need or a sincere desire to know about them. A past life regression is not something to be played with so you can impress other people with who you were, or to create scintillating conversation at a dinner party. It's a serious venture and a wonderful adventure.

The answer to the first question lets me know whether my clients are serious about wanting to explore the events and emotions in their past lives. Most people request a past life regression because of something important that is occurring in their present life—whether it is a relationship drama or a personal problem—that they feel might have its origins in a past life. They want to become aware of that information to help them better understand what is happening to them now and why it is happening. Situations in the present that are related to events and relationships in the past will open up your past life memories because there is a direct connection between the two. Present experiences—and especially your emotions—often trigger spontaneous recall of past life events.

Other people want to have a past life regression because of a sense, either vague or clear, that they need to know something that will help them in their present life, but they're not sure exactly what it is and feel that the answer will be found within a past life event. Still other people are developing their spiritual awareness and a past life regression is another step on their journey to know and understand more about their soul. Some people come for a past life regression to help them discover their purpose in this life and how their present purpose relates to what they've done in past lives.

I ask the second and third questions so that I can help my clients home in on the specific past life that holds the answers and information they are seeking. Many times, in the consultation before the regression, spontaneous memories will begin to surface in the form of insights and intuition that my clients become aware of during the conversation. Knowing as much as possible about why my clients want and need a past life regression will lead to a better session for my clients and encourage more information to come to the surface.

The fourth question shows my clients that they already have a great deal of information about what possibly occurred in their past lives, and that they're ready to become aware of that knowledge so that they can use it to help themselves in their present life. It clarifies the reason why they want a past life regression and shows that they have set goals and expectations for what they want to achieve. This primes their subconscious to bring the past life memories up to the surface.

It also shows that they've devoted a lot of time and soul searching to finding the answer. Everyone knows the truth within. By looking inside yourself, you become aware of what you want to know in a clearer manner, and you set the stage for becoming aware of even more information about the events and emotions contained within situations and relationships in your past lives and you understand how these events and emotions influence and relate to your present life.

Your past life journey will lead you on a spiritual quest for inner truth and knowledge, and will open up your inner awareness. By looking into your past lives, you'll explore who you were, what you've done, and what happened in previous lifetimes, and you'll see how all your experiences have shaped and molded you into who you are now. As you travel into and through your past lives, give yourself the freedom to explore, the curiosity to learn, the challenge to know, and the power to use what you discover. By looking within yourself, within your soul, you'll become aware that you already have all the answers, and you'll find that true knowledge is within. As you look within yourself, trust the insights and information you become aware of.

THE PROCESS AND PURPOSE OF A PAST LIFE REGRESSION

What, exactly, is a past life regression? Will you even be able to recall a past life? What happens during a past life regression? What kind of information comes through, and how does it come to you? What will a past life regression do for you?

A past life regression is your subconscious, spiritual awareness traveling backward through time to access your memories of the events and interconnected emotions that occurred in previous lifetimes. It's accomplished by relaxing your physical body to help you open up and get into your subconscious mind, where you become aware of the events, emotions, relationships, and situations that you experienced in past lives. You hold a wealth of information about the experiences in your past lives within your soul. A past life regression simply opens the doorway to your soul and makes it easier for your soul memories to surface.

Since a past life regression enables you to easily access your soul memories that are housed within your subconscious mind, you can expect to receive information and answers to present problems, and also to find insights into the emotions and experiences in your present life that are reflections of similar events you have experienced in previous lives. A past life regression provides you with information about and an understanding of the experiences you've had and the emotions you've felt, and you become aware of the karma that you've created and carried over into your present life.

During your past life regression, you'll have the opportunity to balance your karma and do a healing on the past life events or emotions, and you'll also be able to resolve and heal past relationships. Because the past and present energies of events and emotions are intertwined, you'll see and feel the effects of the balancing and healing in your present life.

Your soul remembers everything that has ever happened to you in every lifetime. A few of my clients, before their past life regression, worried about whether they'd be able to remember events in their past lives. Let me assure you: Everyone can remember their past lives. The information that surfaces is relevant to what is happening in your present life or is meaningful for your spiritual growth.

There are only four blocks in opening up your memories that you may experience. The first is if you're playing at remembering your past lives and you don't really want to know what happened. You can overcome this through a sincere desire to explore your past lives. The second block is if you doubt your own ability to remember past lives. You can get through this by believing in your ability to remember the events and emotions in your past lives. Simply let go of conscious restrictions that will interfere with your journeys into your past lives. The third block is if you are over-anxious or you try too hard. Past life memories usually surface in a quiet manner with a gentle invitation.

The fourth block occurs when there is serious soul trauma that you experienced in previous lives. You may have a sense that something really bad happened and your fear of knowing what it is may subconsciously prevent a painful past life memory from surfacing. There are two ways through this. The first is to recognize that your soul wants you to become aware of this event or emotion for your spiritual growth; it's always good to know what really happened and why it happened. Your soul may present this information to you in a variety of ways, such as through symbolism and in dreams, to help you deal with it in an easier manner. The second way into and through your fear is by using white light, which will be explained in Chapter Six.

The way that the past life information surfaces varies a great deal from individual to individual. It may either be very dramatic and emotionally charged, completely encompassing your awareness within past life events, as if you are actually there in the scene, reliving and reexperiencing them. Or your past life memories may show themselves in a quiet, gentle manner, as if you're dreaming or watching a movie and seeing the story unfold. You may also experience a combination of the two, feeling emotionally detached as you participate in past life experiences. You may get a clear sense of absolutely knowing about the experiences in your past lives without seeing or feeling the scenes. It depends on what's going on in your present life and how your past life memories and the attached feelings are related to and affect your current experiences. Past life memories come into your conscious mind through your subconscious, more aware, knowing mind.

During your past life regression, you'll feel very relaxed and the information that comes through will be important and relevant to what you are experiencing, or have previously experienced, in your present life, whether it is an emotional trauma, a relationship drama, or an important aspect of knowledge that will guide you to your purpose in this life and help you to evolve your soul. You'll understand the reasons why you have certain experiences in your present life and why you feel the way you do in certain situations.

Getting into your subconscious mind to access your past life memories is easy to do, and is covered in Chapter Four—Rhythm of Relaxing. You need to physically relax your body and quiet your conscious mind for a time to fully open up your subconscious mind and your spiritual awareness. This is where hypnosis comes in.

Hypnosis is an avenue into your subconscious mind where you are receptive to the suggestions that will lead you into opening up your past life memories. It's a method of relaxing your physical body and opening up your subconscious awareness through suggestion and your inherent ability to visualize—to draw pictures from words. When you hear a word, your subconscious automatically and instantaneously changes the word into pictures in your mind, complete with related feelings.

Hypnosis has been around forever and so far no one has yet been able to accurately define it. The best that anyone can come up with is that hypnosis is relaxed receptivity with increased perception, a state of deep relaxation that calms the body, quiets the conscious mind, and opens the subconscious mind through the art of positive suggestions.

The word stems from *hypnos,* which is the Greek word for "sleep." But that's a contradiction in itself. When you're hypnotized, you are definitely not sleeping. While you may appear to be asleep, because your eyes are closed and you're very relaxed, you are much more aware than you are when you're awake. The only way that hypnosis is similar to sleep is that when you are hypnotized, you're in your subconscious mind in much the same way as you are when you are sleeping, except that you're very aware of everything that you're seeing and feeling, and you have excellent recall.

Hypnosis and self-hypnosis are the same thing. All hypnosis is self-hypnosis, whether it involves a hypnotist guiding you or you guiding yourself, because you decide whether or not to accept and act on the suggestions that are given. The only difference is in who is giving the suggestions—the hypnotist or you. The most important thing to keep in mind is that you are always in charge.

While you're engaging in a self-guided past life regression, there are a few key things to keep in mind as you're preparing to regress yourself, setting the tone for your past life trip, and in how you'll be responding to the suggestions. Listen to your feelings as much as you listen to the words. Pay attention to all the subtle nuances of how you're feeling about the suggestions and guidance given. Your subconscious takes everything personally and works on an emotional level.

Your subconscious doesn't hear the unnecessary words in complete sentences. It responds to positive words and phrases that draw the most vibrant, descriptive images, and to words that inspire action or evoke feelings. It will automatically tune out words that aren't important, such as the word *the,* and similar words that it can't form a picture from.

For example, read the following sentence, then close your eyes and repeat the words to yourself. *The little girl played with her puppy.* Your mind will hear the words *little girl, played,* and *puppy.* Your mind will hear and respond to the feelings that these words bring forth. It will draw a very detailed, descriptive picture of a little girl playing with her puppy. It will show you the look on the little girl's face—probably a smile, along with laughter, and will share her feelings with you. You may feel her joy. You'll also see the scene where she is playing with her puppy. What else does that sentence show you and what feelings does it bring forth inside your mind?

Your subconscious mind works by association, as you may have discovered from the little girl/puppy sentence. When you thought that sentence in your mind, you may have seen an image of yourself if you had a puppy when you were a child, or your mind may have showed you a picture of a little girl you'd seen before playing with a puppy. This is the same way your subconscious mind brings forth some of your past life memories, through association with similar scenes and emotions that it pictures from the words you hear and the words you say to yourself.

Try the little girl/puppy sentence a few different ways to see how you respond to the words. *The little girl saw a big dog.* Leaves you kind of lukewarm, doesn't it? Not much emotion or action there. You probably saw a picture of a big dog in your mind, drawn from your memory of what a big dog looks like, maybe walking outside. Perhaps you sensed that the dog was lost. If you were looking through the little girl's eyes, you'd see the big dog from her viewpoint. Maybe you felt her emotions as she looked at the big dog and read her thoughts.

By adding some descriptive action words to the little girl/big dog sentence, your emotions and senses become involved. *The little girl was attacked by a big, ferocious dog.* I'll bet you saw the blood and felt her fear as you watched the dog attack her. You probably wanted to jump into the scene to help her. If you were in the scene, you felt the environment around you, and you may have either traded places with the little girl, experiencing the dog attacking you, or you may have fought off the dog for her. You felt the pain of the dog bites and experienced the fear. Or maybe you envisioned a scene in your mind in which the big dog was either sitting calmly in a fenced-in backyard or was trying to jump the fence. If you were only watching, you may have experienced a sickening feeling in the pit of your stomach.

Here's another sentence: *The little girl snuggled up to the big, furry dog for warmth.* Maybe you saw an image of a little girl lost in the middle of winter with snow all around and night coming on, and you felt grateful for the dog who was keeping her alive. You may even have wanted to organize a search party to find her. These are the same ways you'll respond to the events and emotions inside your past life memories, through the words and suggestions that you either hear or give yourself and by the feelings that are associated with the words and scenes you see in your mind.

Your feelings play a key role in how you access your past life memories. Your subconscious hears, reads, pictures, and responds to your true feelings; your feelings speak louder than words. Your subconscious reads your intentions, as well as the words you hear and the words you say to yourself, as it interprets them and responds accordingly. If you feel even the slightest bit uncomfortable in any manner with the words you're hearing and the simultaneous pictures that the words draw in your mind, or if your feelings don't match the words in the suggestions you're listening to or giving yourself, your subconscious will act on your feelings, rather than the words.

Your belief in yourself, in your ability to open up your past life memories, is a major part in how the memories will surface and what information you will become aware of. If you feel that you can't access your memories, or that you may be making them up and they aren't valid if you do it yourself, you may want to go to a hypnotist to help you open your past life memories. If you decide to go to a hypnotist for a past life regression, here's a checklist of important questions to ask and vital qualities to look for in a hypnotist.

RAPPORT

This is an important quality. Do you like the person who will be hypnotizing you? Does the hypnotist put you at ease and make you feel relaxed? Do you feel absolutely comfortable with this person? You must have a good rapport with the hypnotist you choose. He or she is someone you must trust implicitly. You're not going to let loose with deep, dark, subconscious secrets if you don't like your hypnotist. While you may become aware of them, you might push them away or not let yourself understand them completely because you don't want to share your secrets. You probably won't even allow yourself to be hypnotized because you won't follow the hypnotist's suggestions. You want, and need to have, a complete rapport with and utter confidence in your hypnotist and in his or her ability to guide you into and through your past lives.

Another important consideration is whether the hypnotist you choose is male or female. It may not make any difference to you, but many people prefer a female hypnotist because a woman's voice is softer and her nature tends to be gentle and nurturing. A male hypnotist usually has a more commanding, authoritative presence with a deeper voice that may be a bit intrusive or startling when you're deeply relaxed. Be aware of how you respond to the hypnotist's voice. (For grammatical clarity, I'll refer to a hypnotist in the feminine gender in this section. You can always change the word *she* to *he*.)

QUALIFICATIONS AND/OR CREDENTIALS

Be sure you go to a hypnotist who has been professionally trained. You don't want someone who received her education from a "how-to-do-hypnosis" book or a weekend workshop she attended at the local Y. Ask when she received her certificate of hypnosis and at what school or organization she was trained. Ask if she belongs to the Association for Ethical Hypnosis or another association that adheres to ethical standards. A professional hypnotist will be happy to answer these questions. You want to be professionally and knowledgeably guided, so choose a hypnotist who is qualified. If you become very emotional during your past life regression, a trained hypnotist knows how to handle this.

PROFESSIONALISM

Most important is that you go to a hypnotist who believes in past life regression. This is obvious, but it bears pointing out. Not just any hypnotist will do. Ask how she became interested in hypnosis and why she feels past life regression is important. If she's lukewarm about the subject, she's not for you. If she says she can do a past life regression, even though it isn't something she normally does, it sounds as if she's not entirely enthusiastic and might be more interested in your money than in helping you learn about and understand the events and emotions in your past lives.

ATMOSPHERE

Along with professionalism, consider the setting and atmosphere in which you will be hypnotized. Does she have an office or does she work out of her home? How is her home or office decorated? Do you feel comfortable there? Is her home or office conducive to a past life regression? What is the lighting like? Is there a recliner or a comfortable chair that supports your neck? Is there a couch where you can stretch out? Or does the hypnotist have both so that you have a choice? Most people prefer a recliner as opposed to a couch because they feel more vulnerable lying on a couch.

Do you hear any outside noises, such as traffic or a train, or phones ringing in the office, or people walking by who are talking, or some other noise that may be intrusive? Is the temperature in the room a bit too warm or too cool? What mood does being in the office bring forth in you? While this may be rather intangible, it makes a big difference and is part of the rapport factor. If you're not completely comfortable in her home or office, you're not going to be completely comfortable being hypnotized there and you won't be able to relax.

Ask if she plays soft music or a tape of nature sounds during the regression. This is relaxing for some people and a huge distraction for others. You might tend to focus on the sound rather than focusing on the information contained in your past lives or the sound may lead you in an entirely different direction. For example, if you're hearing the sounds of ocean waves, you may be in a beach scene in your mind. You may also tune out the sound altogether or incorporate it into what you're experiencing in your past life regression. Some hypnotists have a fish tank in their office where you can hear the bubbles in the water and the hum of the motor. Determine if these sounds will bother you or if they are soothing and will relax you even more.

Other hypnotists burn incense to create a mood or light a candle, which may cast shadows that you can see and be aware of, even with your eyes closed. Pay attention to the aromas in the room, including the hypnotist's perfume. How does the smell of the incense affect you? If the candle is scented, do you like the scent? Some people are allergic to strong smells or dislike certain aromas. If you don't like the scent of the incense, or the smoke from it is bothersome, or the scent of the candle or the smell of the hypnotist's cologne, this will make you uncomfortable and distract you from your past life memories.

INDUCTION METHODS
AND THE RIGHT WORDS

Ask about these: It's really, really important. Some hypnotists still use the old school approach to hypnosis. She will instruct you to go down a staircase, counting from one to twenty, tell you to go "deeper, deeper," to enter into "sleep," and wake you up to the count of five with a snap of her fingers. All of this is counterproductive to a past life regression. It's much too regimented and your subconscious mind will reject it.

Your subconscious mind likes to listen to and will respond to a gentle patter of conversation and soft, soothing phrases. Using numbers causes your conscious mind to focus on the numbers, rather than calming it to enable you to enter your subconscious mind, where the past life memories are stored. The whole idea of a past life regression is to calmly quiet your conscious mind, not make it focus, and to lead you gently and naturally into your subconscious mind. The use of the word *sleep* is not appropriate. When you're hypnotized, you're far from sleep; you're very much awake and aware. Make sure the hypnotist uses the word *relax*, *calm*, or *peaceful*, rather than the word *sleep*.

The word *deeper* can be a little tricky, depending on how you respond to it. It's an acceptable word, but may pose some problems for you. If you think that *deeper* and *down* are synonymous, you may close down your awareness. You do want to go deeper into your memory, to travel deeper into your subconscious mind. If you associate the word *deeper* with digging for something that's hard to find or with getting yourself deeper into a problem—maybe to the point where you can't dig yourself out or you're stuck there—avoid the word altogether. It's not so much that you're going deeper into your subconscious as you are heightening your subconscious awareness. Instead of the word *deeper*, your hypnotist could say,

"You're feeling so very relaxed, calm, and peaceful, looking further back in time through your subconscious mind, where you'll find all the memories of your past lives."

This last suggestion, while it seems normal and quite acceptable, will make a *huge* difference in setting the tone for your trip, in how you perceive your past life memories, and the way you experience your regression. If you're "looking further back in time," you'll be an outside observer, watching what happens; if you're "going back in time," you'll be there, actually reexperiencing your past life memories. Just a small change of wording from passively *looking* to actively *going* makes a world of difference. However, once you've accessed your past life memories, the events and emotions contained within them will determine whether you're observing the events or participating in them.

Be careful of the word *down*. If your hypnotist instructs you to go down, she's sending you in the wrong direction. You want to look *up* into the higher aspects of your soul. The word *up* implies opening up; the word *down* implies closing down or shutting off. This is my personal interpretation of these two words. How do you feel about them? The way you feel about them will influence your ability to either open up or close down your past life memories.

While we're on the subject of the interpretation of various words, keep these two things in mind: Your subconscious responds literally to the words that it hears. Your subconscious also responds emotionally to the words that are said. If you don't like the words, or the way they're phrased, you will not accept and respond to the suggestion. You may either rephrase the words in your mind or tune out what the hypnotist is saying altogether.

If you have confidence in the person you choose to hypnotize you, you've already subconsciously agreed to follow her suggestions. *But*, and this is a big *but*, if she says or suggests anything to you that is against your grain, or your core beliefs, or your inner-most desires, you will *not* follow the suggestion. Your subconscious mind will slough it off. You are in control at all times.

Your subconscious likes powerful, vivid words that are phrased in a positive manner. If the hypnotist tells you that you won't be afraid, then you will be afraid. I guarantee it. Your subconscious will hear the word *afraid*, not the preceding words *you won't be*. If she says, "Nothing that you become aware of will hurt you," this suggestion may affect you several ways. You may become aware of nothing. You may focus on the word *hurt* and not go any further. If you accept the suggestion, you'll be missing out on a major part of your past life regression. There are painful, hurtful, traumatic events in everyone's past lives. They can be viewed and experienced in a positive manner so you can see them for what they are and learn from them.

A better way to phrase this suggestion would be, "Everything you become aware of will be beneficial for you in understanding the events and emotions in your past lives, and their relationship to your present life." Your hypnotist should also include a sentence about white light with this suggestion—having previously explained white light to you—that goes something like this: "White light will take care of all the hurt, pain, and any other negatives you may encounter. (We'll get into white light in Chapter Six.)

Is she going to take you down into the deep, dark recesses of your subconscious? Is she going to instruct you to enter an elevator and go down, floor by floor, watching the numbers light up, until the elevator door opens into a past life? I don't know about you, but I hate elevators. I was once attacked and beaten up in an elevator and ended up with a severe head injury. I now avoid elevators; if I have to be in an elevator, I'm extremely apprehensive. If a hypnotist were to instruct me to enter an elevator, once I was relaxed and receptive to suggestions, I would bolt up out of the chair and run right out of her office.

Will your hypnotist instruct you to enter a long hallway with many doors, and tell you that each door opens into a different past life? There are several things wrong with this suggestion. What if you have a sense of claustrophobia about being in a hallway because you feel closed in and can't see any quick means of escape? If you're apprehensive to begin with, you may also feel a fear about opening a certain door because you may pick up intuitive feelings about what is behind it. Compartmentalizing your past lives won't allow you to get into the flow of interrelated events in several past lives.

This is something you need to discuss with your hypnotist. Tell her about any fears, phobias, or bad experiences you've had that might interfere with the suggestions she gives you during your past life regression or the way she instructs you to travel into your past lives. Ask how she phrases her suggestions and tell her the way you would like the suggestions to be worded for you and how you would like to travel into the past. Also, by letting her know about your fears and phobias, you may be helping her to guide you to a past life cause that originated the fear.

Will she take you up into the universe, helping you ascend into the higher aspects of your soul, or will she take you up to the attic in an old house and tell you that your past life memories are stored in an old, dusty trunk? Searching for hidden treasure in an old Victorian mansion might be a fun thing to do on a weekend, but it won't get you very far into your past lives. And what if you're allergic to dust? Your subconscious mind takes everything literally. Do you really want to have a sneezing fit in the hypnotist's office?

Last, but not least, you want to be brought back to the present gently and softly, not rudely jarred into the present with a snap of the hypnotist's fingers. This is extremely startling and is bound to give you a headache, after you were so nicely relaxed, and you'll also lose most of the memory of what you've experienced. Coming back slowly into the present from the past ensures that you retain all of what you experienced, and that you understand it clearly.

Even though I previously stated that hypnosis is not anything like sleep, it can be compared to sleep in the returning/reorienting process. When you wake up to the sound of an alarm clock, you jump out of bed with your heart pounding and it takes a few minutes or more to completely wake up, to get your bearings and orient yourself to where you are. Your dreams are shot into oblivion. When you wake up slowly and naturally from sleep, you feel nice and relaxed, and your dreams are only a thought away. It's the same with returning from a past life journey, except that you have excellent recall.

CONSULTATION

A qualified hypnotist will talk to you on the phone when you first call, or will return your call if you leave a message. She will either offer a free fifteen-minute consultation when you arrive for your appointment or will set up a phone interview. A face-to-face consultation is preferable. Don't get greedy with this. Fifteen minutes is all you need to determine whether the hypnotist is right for you, and for her to gather the information she needs to best help you.

If you've never been hypnotized before, she will explain the process of hypnosis, telling you that basically all hypnosis is self-hypnosis. She'll ask you to practice relaxing by breathing deeply and feeling all the muscles in your body relax, or some other method of becoming calm and quiet, before the appointment to help prime you for the session. She'll also answer any questions you have to put you at ease, and explain how she facilitates a past life regression.

TIME FRAME

Ask how long the past life regression will take. Is she going to regress you into your past lives for forty-five minutes, then pull you out when time is up, no matter what you're experiencing— even if you're in the throes of a death scene—take your money, reschedule you for next week, and usher you out the door, full of questions and concerns? A past life regression needs to be conducted in an atmosphere of peace, with a sense that you—the client—are the most important part of this process.

RATES AND FEES

A reasonable fee for a 1½- to 2-hour past life regression with free consultation is $75 to $100. Some hypnotists may charge upwards of a few hundred dollars, but I'd be a bit leery about this if I were you. A group past life regression in a workshop setting should be $35 to $50. A group regression won't give you individual attention, and you may be rushed into other scenes before you're ready to move on.

Watch out if a hypnotist wants to schedule you for several sessions. One good, lengthy session is all you need to help you open your past life memories. After they're opened, you can take it from there. If you want to continue seeing the hypnotist, you should be charged a lesser fee for her time, since she won't have to go through the complete relaxation/induction method because you'll be familiar with the process, and you'll be able to easily enter a subconscious, more aware frame of mind. You'll also be able to tune in to your past life memories more quickly because you've already established a pathway into the past and opened up your subconscious, spiritual awareness of them.

HEALING

Ask how she goes about helping you to balance your karma and heal the events and emotions in past lives during the regression, or even if that's something she does. Your karma can be balanced in two ways, either immediately during the regression through the energies of your feelings or begun through your feelings during the regression and followed through with positive action in the present. Balancing brings about resolution; healing frees you from negative karma.

It's very important to do a healing on any negativity you become aware of because it's also very important that you not bring negative past life energies back with you into the present. Ask how she clears negative energies. Also ask her about white light. If she doesn't know about white light, walk out the door or hang up the phone immediately. White light is basic and integral to a past life regression. It's used for both protection and healing.

While we're on the subject of spiritual matters and working with past life energies, ask how she handles the interim between lives. Does she cover it at all, only briefly, or in depth? You want a hypnotist who understands the importance of the death scene, crossing over into the interim, and spending some time there to review the past life and to soak up the spiritual vibes. These are important parts of your past life regression and you don't want to miss them!

INTEGRATION

Ask how she will help you understand and connect the experiences and emotions that occurred in your past lives with your present experiences during the regression. Ask how she will help you assimilate and integrate what you've experienced during the regression when you're done. What phrase or suggestion does she use to help you keep remembering events in your past lives after the regression is over? In addition to the consultation before the regression, does she offer you a commentary after your past life regression?

Will she take notes and/or tape-record the regression and offer the notes and tape to you? Many people like to have an audiotape of their past life regression so they can take their time to carefully review what occurred during the session; this helps them bring more associated memories up to the surface, and also triggers other past life memories after the regression that they either didn't become aware of or didn't have time to thoroughly explore. Another big plus is that they can listen to the induction again and go on as many past life journeys as they'd like.

Pros and Cons

When you go to a hypnotist, you're trusting that she will correctly guide you during your past life regression and that she is experienced and knowledgeable about hypnosis and past life regression. Going to a hypnotist may be helpful for people who feel they can't or don't want to do it themselves. Or perhaps they believe that what they become aware of isn't real unless it's validated by an outside source—a hypnotist. Some people feel they can't access the information, and going to a hypnotist assures them that the memories will open up. If you feel this way, by all means engage the services of a qualified hypnotist to help you open up your past life memories.

While this book is about how to do a complete past life regression for yourself, and various other ways to access your past life memories, going to a hypnotist may give you a greater advantage.

If your hypnotist is tuned in to what you're experiencing during your regression, she can guide you in a one-on-one manner that is most appropriate for you to fully experience and explore what you become aware of in your past life memories, and she may also be able to provide you with valuable insights.

Keep this in mind, too. You can accomplish all this while guiding yourself through your past lives. If, at any time during your past life regression, you want to more fully explore what you are experiencing and feel that you are being rushed through something, simply pause and give yourself quiet time to get as deeply into your memory as you desire.

As you'll discover a bit later in this book, you'll have your own intuitive, inner guide. You'll be establishing a soul rapport with your higher self, who is your inner guide. You'll meet your higher self, if you haven't already, in Chapter Eight. Your higher self, who knows everything about you and all your past life memories, knows how to best guide you because, for all intents and purposes, you're guiding yourself and giving yourself insights and answers from a heightened level of soul awareness.

By doing your own past life regression, you know that you have the power within you to open up your past life memories and you trust your ability to do so. Your confidence will inspire your subconscious mind to open up and show you all the descriptive details and emotions in moving pictures of your past life memories, and will provide you with a complete, comprehensive understanding of all that you experience.

3

IMPRINTS AND
IMPRESSIONS OF YOUR
PAST LIVES

A past life regression isn't the only way to discover your past lives. Before we begin the actual journey into your past lives, there are many other ways you can remember and get a good sense about your previous incarnations without engaging in a past life regression. A tremendous amount of information comes to you in your dreams, in what appears to be random thoughts and reveries, through your intuition, in images that flash into your mind, through purposeful meditation, and through déjà vu feelings, as well as when you have a hunch or a sense about events you experienced in your past lives.

When you pay attention to and get further involved with the preliminary information you become aware of, it will trigger more information and provide you with ways to explore the events and emotions in your past lives. Information that comes through in your dreams and meditations, and in feelings related to a past life, are given to you by your subconscious, which is your soul—your spiritual awareness.

You can recognize past life influences in the present. The imprints and impressions of experiences in your past lives are etched into your soul and mirrored in similar present day experiences that reflect past life events and emotions. Repetitions and reappearances from the past are all around you because the energies of past events interweave through time into the present.

Look into the situations in your life that replay themselves in slightly different versions; they're often influenced by events and emotions that you experienced in past lives. They show you how your karma is playing out and what you've carried over—both good and bad. You can trace the past life memory through what is occurring in the present by paying attention to your feelings about it. Follow your feelings and your inner sense of spiritual knowing to lead you into the interconnected past life memory.

The vibrations of past life energies may show up in the present in seemingly chance encounters and coincidences that you've drawn to yourself for your soul to experience. You may also experience them as serendipity, something that occurs when everything falls into place perfectly. They may show up as luck, or being in the right place at the right time. Before birth into this lifetime, you created and chose to have certain experiences that will evolve your soul. When they begin to happen in your life, you remember them on a soul level.

You may already be aware of some of the events and emotions you experienced in past lives without consciously knowing that you're aware of them. They may be just below the surface of your subconscious, maybe as a feeling or an image, waiting only for your recognition. They show up all the time in your present life, sometimes in small ways, at other times appearing in a dramatic fashion.

Pieces of your past life experiences may appear in flashbacks, where you have a momentary remembrance of a significant event, and in fleeting glimpses and random images that appear out of the clear blue sky in your thoughts and feelings. They usually appear when something in your present life—a feeling or a situation—is similar to something you experienced in a past life. These feelings and fleeting images can open doorways and windows—other avenues of awareness—into more clearly seeing and expanding your memories so you can explore every aspect and facet of them.

When you're beginning to look for present reflections of the past, you may simply get a sense of something, a general knowing or awareness, or perhaps an intuitive feeling. Give this glimpse or fleeting feeling room to grow. Honor your feeling by allowing it to happen at the best and most appropriate time. Don't demand that it appear immediately in a way that clearly shows itself. You'll lose it if you force it. Let it play gently on your mind, similar to how you ponder a vague dream image before it becomes apparent.

For example, you may get a feeling that you lived in a jungle with no other information. Three days later, you get a stronger sense that you were a male. With that sense, you catch a glimpse in your mind's eye of someone with dark skin dressed in a loin-cloth and carrying a spear. That night you dream about that person and in your dream you remember more information about his/your past life. As time goes by, more information comes to you in your thoughts and feelings; perhaps you become aware of the purpose in that life and the reasons you've remembered that incarnation by seeing how it relates to your present life.

Sometimes the feelings you become aware of are rather generic. Madeline, one of my students, said she felt as if she were being smothered in her job and felt claustrophobic at work. Her office was a little cubbyhole with no windows, but she felt it went deeper than that. She was also having problems with her boss, who was not giving her ideas the attention and appreciation she felt they deserved. She meditated on her feelings to see if there was a connection between a past life and what she was experiencing now. She remembered a lifetime with her boss when he was her husband and had smothered her by not allowing her to voice her feelings or opinions. In this life, she's experiencing the same feeling of being smothered and unappreciated in a slightly different manner.

If you have feelings that you can't quite put your finger on, such as feeling really good or bad in some of your present situations and not completely understanding why you feel that way, or reacting to something in an uncharacteristic manner, you could be responding to an emotion contained within a consciously forgotten past life memory that is influencing you; your feelings and reactions are brought about by similarities in the situations.

These fleeting feelings and glimpses will continue to open up your past life memories in your thoughts and feelings during the day, in your dreams at night, and through meditation. Once you've opened up the desire to remember experiences in your past lives, you've opened the space, or energy vibration, for them to come through as related issues arise in your present life. All you have to do is recognize the past life influences to see how and when the past shows itself in the present.

You may also experience the past showing up in the present in a powerful moment of absolutely clear knowing about an event in one of your past lives. This is spontaneous recall and can be very dramatic because it's triggered by a closely related present-day event or is brought forth by an intense emotion that is quite similar to what you experienced in the past.

CURRENT CONNECTIONS

Past life memories show up in the present in a variety of ways. Scenes that are reminiscent of places you've lived in past lives may trigger your memories. One of my friends went to Scotland with her husband on a business trip. The moment she arrived, memories flooded into her mind of when she had lived there before in a past life with her husband. Everything was familiar to her; she knew her way around without asking directions.

One of my students has always felt drawn to Egypt. She was seriously into pyramid power in the '70s; she even named her dog Pharaoh and her cat Sphinx. She went to the museum when the Egyptian exhibit was on display. When she saw the artifacts, memories of a lifetime in Egypt spontaneously surfaced. She was so inspired by what she saw and remembered that she booked a tour of Egypt. While she was there, memories of her past lifetime opened up in great detail.

You may feel drawn to a particular place because your soul may need to experience something there for growth and learning or because there is someone there from a past life whom you need to meet. At a book fair, a woman came over to my table to look at my book on psychic awareness and started a conversation. She told me that she had been living in another state and was quite happy there, but felt an irresistible, intuitive pull to move. She followed her feeling and met her husband. She said the moment she met him, she knew they'd been together before. Her soul was guiding her to where she needed to be to reunite with her soulmate.

Maybe you've felt an instant attraction to or an immediate dislike for someone you've just met. It's very likely that you knew this person in a past life. Your soul remembers him or her even if you don't. How often have you felt, with another person you've just met, that you were picking up where you left off, that you were continuing something that was already begun? And that the time between being with this person seemed as if it were only yesterday instead of a lifetime ago? More information is given on past/present people in Chapter Nine.

Look at what is around you every day; notice your feelings and responses to everyday items and situations that may seem ordinary at first glance, yet may turn out to be quite significant. When you look further into them, you may see clues into who you were and what you did in your past lives. In my first book on reincarnation, *Discovering Your Past Lives*, there was an in-depth current clues questionnaire to help readers find connections to their past lives in their present life. The following are some of the highlights, and your soul may resonate with them.

Your current lifestyle may show you how the past is influencing you. The things you enjoy doing and feel comfortable with could be things you've done and enjoyed before. If you have a talent or a flair for doing certain things, or you've always wanted to pursue a certain interest or hobby, your desire could reflect a lifetime where you've begun or enjoyed this before. Your preference or dislike for certain ethnic foods might be a clue to where you've lived in past lives. Your home and the way you decorate it may resonate with places you've lived before. Your career could be a continuation of a past life career. If you really love what you're doing and you're good at it, it's a pretty sure bet you've done it before.

While you're looking in the present to find the past, look into yourself. Some of your personality traits and the little quirks that make you uniquely you may be influenced by who you were in past lives. Look at your fears and phobias. If you can't pinpoint a present cause, they may be due to something in a past life. Past life emotions carry over very strongly, sometimes without the corresponding memory. This may explain why you react in an uncharacteristic manner in certain situations or to other people.

Your health can show you things about what you experienced in your past lives. Your karma relating to your health may be symbolic of actions and attitudes in past lives; you may have chosen to experience a health problem to learn particular lessons or gain certain qualities such as empathy or compassion. Birthmarks may indicate past life injury or trauma to that particular area. For example, if you have a birthmark on your neck, you may have been hung in a past life. Aches and pains that seem to come out of nowhere, for no apparent reason and without a cause in the present, may be due to past life influences.

Current connections provide you with insights into what you experienced and what you were like in past lives. Echoes from the past replay themselves in present problems and situations that have their origins in past lives. If you've ever wondered why you feel strongly about particular things or certain people, without understanding the specific reason in the present, look to a past life event to find out why. Be receptive to seeing past life influences that are reflected in your present feelings, situations, relationships, and experiences. Look for similarities to make the connection.

INTUITION—YOUR INNER KNOWING

You can further open up the imprints and impressions of your past lives by honoring your hunches and opening up your insights and inner knowings—your intuition—and by tuning in to your spiritual awareness. Your intuition is an inborn, innate ability. You were born with your spiritual knowing; you can tune in to it and turn it on at any time. You can intuitively see through the surface of your current experiences to see the reflections of related past life events.

You can use your intuition to see through and understand the fleeting glimpses and thoughts which float through your mind that you feel are about something in your past lives. Your soul remembers and will share this information with you. You can go within your inner knowing—your spiritual awareness—to become aware of how the past shows itself in the present. Trust your feelings and what you know inside to be true. Your insights and inner knowing—your intuitive awareness—will show you sights from your past lives in the following side trip. You already know, inside your subconscious, what happened in your past lives.

SIDE TRIP . . . INTUITIVE INSIGHTS

This easy, do-it-yourself meditation will open up many pieces of your past lives. It may provide you with a full-blown account of a past life or give you a starting point for what you'll experience in your past life regression. It focuses on similar experiences and situations between the past and the present. This is the interweaving energy—the connecting thread—that you'll follow from the present into the past.

> Take a deep breath and just let yourself relax. Let go of all the tension and tightness in your body. Let your conscious mind become calm and quiet. Breathe naturally and normally for a few minutes as your body relaxes. As you relax and become centered within yourself, you'll enter a meditative frame of mind. Think about a current situation or problem that you feel might be connected to or related to something in a past life. Focus on your feelings and on what is happening in the present to lead you into the past. Open up your intuition—your inner knowing—to show you related past life events and emotions that are similar to what you're experiencing now.

Let the past life scenes appear in your mind. Let yourself sense them and become aware of them. Tune in to the feelings you felt before in the past. See and be completely involved in everything that is happening; let yourself see and be in the scenes from your past life as you feel your emotions and listen to your thoughts. Go with the flow of your insights and the intuitive information that appears in your mind.

Look for similarities between the past life events and your present experiences to understand how and why the past influences and affects what you're currently experiencing in the present. Connect how the information you receive about a past life fits into your present life. Just let this information come to you in the course of your meditation. When you're done, come back slowly into the present, bringing with you the awareness of all that you've remembered about the events and emotions in your past life. Reflect on all the images you saw, and your thoughts and feelings about everything you've become aware of.

DÉJÀ VU AND DREAMS

You can remember events and emotions in your past lives through déjà vu. Déjà vu is a feeling of having been somewhere before, having seen something before, or of reliving something you've previously experienced. It literally means "already seen." You may have had many feelings about or remembrances of events in your past lives through feelings of déjà vu.

Many present events and emotions are reminiscent of similar events and emotions in your past lives. Déjà vu is triggered by the similarities between the past and present situations and feelings. You may have responded to a situation with an uncanny feeling that this has occurred before without knowing exactly where or when you've had the experience, and without recalling the specific past life event.

One of my students found himself in a déjà vu situation that brought the beginnings of a past life memory to the surface. He was on his way to a New Age bookstore that he'd never been to before to attend a workshop. It was a long distance from his home and he was following the directions when he saw a park beyond some trees in his peripheral vision that was just off the street. His heart started pounding and he immediately felt strongly drawn to the park, so he stopped his car and went to explore. As he walked around the park, he had a sense that he'd experienced a similar scene before, along with a feeling of dread.

He sensed that there was more to this place that seemed so familiar to him. He knew, without any doubt, that he'd been there before. The memory tugged at his mind. Then he remembered. In a past life, the park had been a field he'd been running through, trying to get to his farmhouse as it was burning. His heart started pounding again as he reexperienced the fear he'd felt before, running as fast as he could to save his wife and small daughter in that lifetime.

Déjà vu isn't always an earth-shattering experience; most of the time it appears quietly and almost imperceptibly with a vague feeling of knowing something without knowing how you know it. When you give your déjà vu feelings your full attention, and open up your intuitive awareness, the past life memory comes through.

Feelings of déjà vu can also be brought about by a dream you've had. Pictures of your past lives pop up all the time in your dreams. Perhaps you dreamed about events in a past life, then consciously forgot the dream or thought it was meaningless. When something in your present life triggers a remembrance of the dream as a feeling of déjà vu, use that feeling to bring the events in the dream into your conscious awareness.

Dreams occur in your subconscious mind, where your past life memories are also stored. They provide you with connections and show you pictures from your past lives. Dreams are a doorway that bridge the past and the present. They show events and emotions from your past lives, as well as giving you insights into and information about present experiences. Some past life dreams show clear images of who you were before and the things you experienced; they portray past life scenes that relate directly to your present life. These dreams explain the relationship between what you're currently experiencing and what you experienced in a past life.

Other dreams show related fragments of past life pictures; they may include people you're currently involved with whom you shared a past life with. The dream replays events you experienced with them that are now affecting you, and may also show you the karma, either literally or symbolically, that needs to be balanced. Some of your dreams may show present situations that are similar to past life experiences; you dream about past events in a present time frame and in a present setting. Look for similarities or connections to present situations that may be reflections of past life events.

Some of your past life dreams are easy to interpret because the dreams are literal and the images are clear. If your dreams are a bit difficult to understand, they could be showing you emotions and events from your past lives that you're not yet ready to become fully aware of and accept, and you may need to further discover and explore the images that your dreams offer you.

Determine if your dreams are about your past lives, or if they relate only to your present life, by looking at the overall message and feeling in your dreams. Connect your past life dreams with the events, emotions, and experiences in your present life. Pay attention to your feelings about your dreams. A past life dream shows itself in many different ways. Your feelings will help you determine the dreams that show you the pictures of your past lives.

You can make past life dreams happen. Before you go to sleep, tell yourself that you'll dream about a past life. Your subconscious will select the past life that is most appropriate for you to become aware of. If you already have some information about one of your past lives, incorporate it into your suggestion. If you have a problem in your present life that you feel relates to a past life, put that into the mix. As you're programming your dream, you may become aware of an image or a feeling about a past life. This is your subconscious mind tuning in to one of your past lives and giving you a preview of coming attractions.

One of my students, Maggie, told me about a dream she had that led to exploring a soul connection with her boyfriend, David. The only thing that was clear in her dream was a word she'd never heard before. When she looked up the word, and began to explore the past life that the word opened up, it led to a very dramatic past life event.

The word was *Antigua*. The dictionary told her it was an island in the West Indies, but that didn't feel quite right to her. Upon further research, she discovered that there was also an Antigua in Guatemala. With that information, she saw a picture in her mind's eye of an oval opening in the face of a rock. Looking through a tourist brochure of Guatemala, she saw that same rock. During the next several weeks, more information about that lifetime came to her. Through meditating, she began to see images of her past life there and to remember events she'd been involved in. She knew she'd lived there before with her boyfriend and that something bad had happened between them.

One night when they were together during a thunderstorm, she had a flash of knowing that she had stabbed him in the back with a dagger in a past life. The stabbing had occurred during a thunderstorm in that past life. At the same moment she became aware of this, her boyfriend said his back hurt. She touched a spot on his back and asked him if this was where it hurt. He said yes; it was the same spot where she had stabbed him in a previous lifetime. Needless to say, she was a little freaked out about this and didn't tell David that she had stabbed him in a past life. Their relationship had been going quite well but after that night, he began avoiding her.

During my reincarnation class several weeks later, I mentioned that a person's eyes were the window to their soul and that you could see into another person's soul by staring into his or her eyes over the flame of a candle. Maggie decided to do this and invited David over. She told him about the candle meditation and explained that she thought they'd been together in a past life and wanted to see inside his soul. He agreed to it, so she lit a candle and placed it on the table between them. She had a pencil and notebook to write down the information that came through.

David wasn't taking all of this seriously and was making jokes about the pencil. He asked her if she was going to stab him with it. She didn't say anything but wondered if he had the same soul memories that she did. As they stared into each other's eyes, he remembered all the things and more that she had become aware of in the last few weeks. He knew that she had stabbed him with a dagger. His memories confirmed what she already knew, what she had first become aware of through a word that appeared in a dream.

If you'd like to do a candle meditation with someone you feel you were with in a past life, here's how: This meditation is very serious; it's important to approach it in a respectful manner. It can get a little spooky; you may become a bit frightened by what you see in another person's eyes and in the facial features as they change if you're not prepared for it. Staring into someone's eyes will provide you with a tremendous amount of information about shared experiences.

At first, you'll see your partner's face as he/she looks in this lifetime, the way he/she appears every day. Focus on the eyes and pay attention to your thoughts and feelings as you're looking into his/her eyes and at his/her face. As you're looking into his/her eyes, you'll both move past the physical appearance and see the images of his/her face as he/she appeared in previous incarnations. The person's eyes will change; you'll feel as if you're looking at someone else. You'll also see different facial features become superimposed over his/her face. You may feel as if he/she isn't who he/she is now, and you may also feel as if you aren't who you are now; it's a rather distinct, somewhat eerie feeling. The vibes or atmosphere in the room will also feel different.

Before you begin, you should both enter a meditative frame of mind and surround yourselves with white light. (White light will keep the vibes on a spiritual level, and will protect you from experiencing any negativity. White light is covered in Chapter Six.) Light a candle and place it between you. Keep the lights on in the room. Sit across a table from him or her and hold hands. This forms both a physical and a telepathic link between you. Look deeply into each other's eyes to see his/her soul and tell the person what you see and sense. This helps you become more aware of your spiritual connection with him or her, and will also trigger insights for the other person. Additionally, each of you will become aware of past life experiences you've shared.

This candle meditation is one avenue into remembering events and emotions in your past lives that you experienced with another person. If you'd like to do a candle meditation by yourself to see into and through your soul, to become aware of experiences in past lives, light a candle and look into a mirror at your eyes and face. Pay attention to the thoughts and feelings that come to you as well as what you see.

Present and Past Life Purposes/Discovering Your Dreams

In addition to remembering information about your past lives through your dreams, they can help you in every part of your present life. Dreams occur in your subconscious, in the realm of your inner knowing. They open up your spiritual awareness and share the secrets of your soul with you. Pay attention to your dreams. Make a daily habit of remembering them. They may be showing you pictures of your past lives or helping you in many other ways in your present life.

PART II

VIBRATIONS

4

RHYTHM OF RELAXING

etting into your subconscious mind to gain access to
your past life memories is the first part of your past
life regression. It's a natural process and is easy to do:
All you have to do is physically relax. By simply letting your body
completely relax from head to toe, you automatically enter your
subconscious mind. Physical relaxation is a very gentle rhythm
that is in harmony with your mind's awareness. As you physically
relax, all the tension and tightness in your body flows away from
you, as your conscious mind simultaneously frees itself from all
your everyday thoughts, cares, and worries. As a natural feeling of
relaxation replaces body tension, all the muscles in your body
relax, and you clear out the clutter and quiet the chatter from your
conscious mind.

As your conscious mind becomes calm and quiet, which is a
natural by-product of physical relaxation, you focus your awareness into your subconscious mind, into the spiritual place of
knowing awareness within you, and you enter a meditative frame
of mind where you have access to your past life memories. Being

in a meditative frame of mind feels very peaceful, like a flowing, rhythmic sensation where you're in tune with yourself and in harmony with your spiritual essence.

You've done this many times before, maybe not with the purpose of traveling through time to remember your past lives, but instead just simply to relax after a long, hard, busy day of working or running errands to get into your own vibes. Maybe you sat in a comfortable chair or laid down on a soft couch, closed your eyes, and let your body relax as you cleared your conscious mind by letting go of the thoughts of the day. Maybe you daydreamed, going somewhere pleasant in your mind. When you're feeling relaxed and comfortable, mellow and peaceful, you're also tuning in to yourself, in to your true feelings, and in to your spiritual awareness. It's the same with the first step on your past life journey.

Stretch out on a couch or sit in a comfortable chair that completely supports your neck and back. Uncross your legs and let your hands rest at your side. Just breathe naturally and normally as you begin to let your body relax, as you begin to feel your body gently relaxing, and as you let your thoughts go and allow your conscious mind to become calm and quiet. Just breathe. Just let yourself relax. Just let your thoughts go. Gently focus your awareness on your breathing. Your breathing will relax you and quiet your conscious mind as you direct your attention inward toward the more aware, knowing part of you, toward your spiritual awareness.

Close your eyes and get into the rhythm of relaxing. Take your time and go slowly, feeling and experiencing every sensation completely in the present moment. Begin to relax your body, and to clear and calm your conscious mind by breathing naturally, by breathing deeply. Just let it happen. Relaxation is a very pleasant feeling of peacefulness, a lovely feeling of harmony, of being in tune with yourself. Take a deep breath in and let it out slowly. Focus your attention and awareness on your breathing for a few minutes. Just breathe. Notice how the simple act of breathing begins to relax you; notice how calm you're beginning to feel.

Listen to the sound of your breathing as you breathe in and out, slowly and naturally. Listen to your breathing as you're feeling your body relax, as you're letting your conscious mind become calm and quiet as you center your awareness within yourself. Just breathe. As you're breathing in, imagine that you're inhaling positive, relaxing feelings, allowing a gentle, peaceful feeling of relaxation to flow softly into and through you, feeling it circulating through you in a gentle rhythm of harmony and relaxation, a gentle feeling of peacefulness and well-being. As you're breathing out, imagine that you're exhaling negative thoughts and feelings, simply letting go of all your cares, worries, or problems in an easy, carefree manner, releasing all your thoughts and feelings from your everyday experiences as you allow your breathing to ease all the tension and tightness from your body.

Breathe in the harmony. Breathe out the mind chatter. Breathe in a feeling of relaxation and well-being. Breathe out all body tensions and unnecessary thoughts that crowd your conscious mind, as you turn your attention inward toward your subconscious mind, toward the past life memories that you want to open up and explore.

By first beginning to relax your body with a few deep breaths, you cleanse your lungs and clear your mind. As your conscious mind becomes calm and quiet, and your body becomes more comfortable and relaxed, you tune out the physical world for a time as you tune in to a subtle, more aware, inner level of mind. By directing and focusing your attention and awareness inward, you open up your subconscious mind and enter a meditative, more aware, spiritual frame of mind.

Breathe. Just breathe. Simply feel a gentle flow of relaxation drifting slowly and softly down into and through your entire body. Breathe in positive, relaxing feelings; breathe out negative thoughts and feelings. Breathe in the relaxation. Breathe out the tension. Breathe in the calmness and the quiet. Breathe out the noise and the disturbances. Breathe in the relaxation. Feel it softly and naturally flowing into you and through you, filling you with perfect peace and harmony. Feel all your muscles beginning to relax as they let go of all the tension and tightness in your body.

Feel the peaceful feeling of relaxation flowing through your entire body, feeling every part of your body becoming totally relaxed and comfortable from the top of your head all the way down through the tips of your toes. Breathe in and out, gently, softly, naturally. Feel your mind become calm and quiet. Feel peaceful and centered within yourself. Relaxing your body, opening up your subconscious mind, and focusing your attention and awareness inward is a gentle, flowing process, a soothing rhythm and motion. It's as easy and natural as breathing.

By focusing your attention inward, you begin to see and sense your past life images as you open up your subconscious awareness and enter a meditative, more aware frame of mind. Let your subconscious mind move at its own rate and follow your own pace. Just relax and let your thoughts go. Focus on your breathing as you feel a gentle flow of peaceful relaxation drifting softly into and through your entire body. Breathe. Just breathe. You can interact with and influence your level of relaxation simply through your breathing. Let your breathing relax your body, calm and quiet your conscious mind, and open up your inner awareness. Let your breathing bring you into a peaceful, calm, quiet place within yourself.

Just breathe for a few moments, letting yourself become even more relaxed, letting yourself feel completely calm, quiet, and peaceful. If you'd like, completely stretch out on your couch or move around in your comfortable chair so you feel completely comfortable where you are and your body feels completely relaxed. Breathe some more and get into the rhythm of relaxing. Just focus on your breathing.

Breathe. Just breathe. Notice how the simple act of breathing relaxes you; notice how calm and quiet you're feeling. Let a gentle flow, a soothing, peaceful feeling of relaxation drift slowly and softly down into and through your entire body. Breathe in positive, relaxing feelings; breathe out negative thoughts and feelings. As you're breathing in and out in harmony with yourself, let this soft, easy, peaceful feeling of relaxation gently and naturally flow all the way through you, calming your conscious mind and replacing body tension. Feel all the muscles and cells, nerves and tissues—every part of your body—relaxing from the top of your head all the way down through the tips of your toes.

Feel this calming, soothing, gentle, natural, very peaceful feeling of relaxation flowing deeply down into and through your body, into and through every part of you, beginning at the top of your head. Feel this soothing, peaceful flow of relaxation that is in harmony with your breathing as a very gentle feeling that flows slowly and softly all the way down into and through you, descending gradually through all the muscles in your forehead and your face, relaxing the muscles around your eyes, your nose, your mouth, and your jaw.

Breathe naturally as you allow your breathing to relax you even more. Let this very peaceful, calming, soothing feeling of relaxation— this gentle rhythm—flow slowly and softly down into and through your neck and your shoulders, gently easing all the tension, letting it just drift away, replacing it with a soft, natural, peaceful feeling of gentle relaxation that flows all the way down into and through your back, vertebra by vertebra, loosening and letting go of all the tension and tightness from the muscles in your back.

As this gentle feeling, this rhythm of relaxation, flows softly and slowly all the way down into and through your chest and abdomen, you'll notice that as your stomach muscles relax, your breathing becomes deeper and slows to a more regular, natural rhythm that is in harmony with your level of relaxation. Listen to your breathing as you breathe in and out. Listen to your breathing, feeling so very peaceful within yourself.

Now that you're feeling much more relaxed, maybe you'd like to move around a little bit, to readjust your position and get even more comfortable. If you want to, take a moment to gently stretch and then relax even more deeply, now that you've let go of all the tension and tightness from your face and jaw, your neck and shoulders, and from your back, chest, and abdomen.

Sinking deeper into the couch or comfortable chair, letting it completely support your body, continue to breathe naturally, feeling this peaceful, gentle, soft, easy rhythm of relaxation flow slowly and naturally down from your shoulders into and through your arms, elbows, wrists, hands, and fingers.

Just breathing, feeling the gentle flow of relaxation circulate softly and rhythmically through your body. You feel so deeply relaxed now. Peaceful. Quiet. Soothed, as the soft, easy feeling of relaxation continues to flow gently down from your stomach and your back into and through your hips, thighs, knees, calves, ankles, feet, and toes.

You're so comfortable and your body is so completely relaxed. You're feeling perfectly relaxed and peaceful within yourself, in harmony with your subconscious mind, completely in tune with your spiritual awareness. Enjoy your calm, quiet, peaceful feeling of relaxation for a while. Just breathe and be, feeling completely comfortable, perfectly relaxed. Enjoy the pleasant feeling of just being.

When your physical body is relaxed, and your conscious mind is calm and quiet, you're inside your subconscious mind—you're in a much more aware, meditative frame of mind—a spiritual place of knowing where you can open up your past life memories and explore them.

SIDETRACKS . . .
Present Purposes

There are many wonderful benefits to relaxing that aren't related to remembering your past lives, but that directly affect your present life in many positive, beneficial ways. By simply relaxing, physical changes occur naturally within your body that affect your health and well-being. You reduce stress and relieve tension and fatigue, as you refresh and replenish yourself in body, mind, and spirit. When you're relaxed, your breathing and heart rate slow to a natural, peaceful rhythm, and your internal organs are affected in gentle, healing ways. Your cells and muscles eliminate toxins and cleanse themselves. As you relax, your body releases endorphins that increase your physical and mental well-being; these endorphins also contribute to your health.

As your conscious mind becomes calm and quiet, your brain wave pattern slows from a beta rhythm, which is your everyday, waking, conscious level, to an alpha rhythm, which is a more aware, inner, subconscious level of mind. As you enter a more aware level of mind, you enjoy many metaphysical benefits of opening up and expanding your inner awareness, of being in tune with yourself and in touch with your true feelings. You enter a place within yourself where you can clearly think, and where you can meditate.

You create and enjoy a more positive attitude and a better frame of mind. You open a channel of communication between your conscious and subconscious mind that will help you in any way you desire. You open up your natural abilities to visualize—to see with your mind's eye—and to intuitively feel with your inner senses. You open yourself up to your inner knowing and to experiencing your spiritual awareness.

SIDE TRIP ... HEALING AND HARMONIZING YOUR BODY, MIND, AND SPIRIT

There is a very special, spiritual way to use your breathing and body relaxation to bring health and harmony to your body, mind, and spirit, and to increase your spiritual awareness. The way to do this is to breathe in the essence and feeling of a white light vibration, which is a universal source of energy that is both protective and healing. This white light will be used in several ways throughout the book.

For the moment, you can incorporate white light into your relaxation to do one or all of the following: You can just enjoy it, you can use it to raise your level of spiritual awareness, and you can allow white light to heal you in whatever way you desire. Simply breathe the essence and feeling of white light inside you, letting it flow into and through your body, mind, and spirit. That is all you need to do. White light will take care of the rest.

> Breathe in a very peaceful, spiritual, pure, cleansing white light that calms and quiets your conscious mind as it softly flows into and through you, completely relaxing you. This beautiful light heals and harmonizes every part of your body as it gently circulates all around you, like a soft and gentle breeze, as it flows within and through you, like a rhythmic heartbeat. Breathe in the wonderful essence and peaceful feelings of this white light; feel the light breathing in harmony with you.

You may also want to picture yourself or feel yourself in a beautiful, lush green garden that is flowing with vibrant health and harmony as you breathe in this wonderful image, feeling, and essence of white light. Perhaps you perceive white light as rays of sunlight, shining brightly all around you, permeating your body with the gentle warmth and light-energy of the sun as it flows into and through your body, mind, and spirit.

Breathe in the pure, positive, peaceful vibrations of universal white light into your body, mind, and soul. Allow white light to calm, quiet, and clear your conscious mind, to softly and naturally relax your body, to open up your spiritual awareness, and to heal you in every way. Feel the gentle, harmonious, healing vibrations of white light circulate and flow softly and slowly into and through your body, mind, and spirit. Breathe in this wonderfully beneficial white light to open up your subconscious awareness— your inner knowing—and to show you your true spiritual nature, the essence of your soul.

The peaceful energy essence and feelings of white light are very special, positive, and powerful. Your body, mind, and soul are in tune with the harmony and spiritual/universal vibrations of white light. Your body, mind, and soul resonate perfectly and naturally with the healing vibrations and peaceful essence of white light. It is one of the many gifts that your soul-mind gives to you. It is your spiritual birthright.

RISING THROUGH
THE RAINBOW

To continue with your past life regression, remain relaxed as you journey through a magical, mystical rainbow in your mind. Before you go into your past life memories, you'll be rising through the seven colors of a rainbow. By rising through the energies of the colors to the top of the rainbow, you enter an even more aware frame of mind, where you're in touch with and in tune with yourself on an inner, spiritual level.

As you ascend through the colors of the rainbow—beginning at the bottom with red, then rising into orange, yellow, green, blue, indigo (a deep purplish-blue), and violet—take your time inside each color to completely enjoy, experience, and absorb the color within your body and your mind. Experience the unique energies and vibrations of each color; feel their rhythm and harmony. Breathe the colors inside you. Be the colors inside you. See, feel, and sense the vibrations of each color as you go inside and through the magical, mystical rainbow in your mind.

As you're traveling through the rainbow, you might see or sense an image or a scene inside each color. You may become aware of feelings within each color that will be beneficial and helpful to you. Take your time to explore these images and feelings; they may be offering you a way into your past life memories, or helping you in some other special way that is important and meaningful. Perhaps you'll see a scene involving several images that move and change as you become aware of them, or perhaps you'll focus entirely on feeling the vibrations of each color.

Accept what you see and feel. Your subconscious speaks to you in symbols and imagery; it's the language of your mind. By accepting the pictures and feelings that your mind offers you in the way that they are presented to you, you're opening up your subconscious mind even more and tuning in to your true spiritual nature. The images you see and the feelings you experience inside each color of the rainbow will be meaningful for you in a very special way. The vibrations of each color will offer you increased awareness.

As you continue to breathe naturally, feeling perfectly relaxed and peaceful, perfectly calm and quiet within yourself, imagine an early morning rainfall. Listen to the sound of the rain as it gently taps on your window. The sound is lulling and soothing, comforting and relaxing. As the soft, steady rhythm of the rain continues, you feel peaceful and quiet within yourself. Just enjoy this feeling for a while.

The raindrops begin to patter slowly now as the rain softly comes to an end. Looking outside, through the window, you notice that the sky is beginning to clear and you see the sun beginning to emerge from behind white, misty clouds that are floating leisurely through the sky. Opening up the window, you feel the pleasant warmth of the summer day and decide to go outside to enjoy the warmth and light of the sun.

As you step outside, everything looks bright and beautiful. Breathe in the freshness of the gentle breeze and the wonderful scent of the wet earth. Experience the wonderful, refreshing feeling of a rain shower that has just ended. Looking up at the sky, you notice the most beautiful rainbow you've ever seen. The rainbow has been formed by the early morning rainfall and by the sunshine that filters through the soft, misty clouds. The colors of the rainbow are vibrant and pure, a shimmering spectrum of colors that blend into one another, vibrating perfectly in tune with each other, creating harmony within your mind and soul.

It's the most beautiful rainbow you've ever seen. It surrounds you like a perfect dome that touches the earth and the sky. You feel as if you could reach up and touch the rainbow. You feel as if you could breathe in the colors and be inside them. You feel as if you could rise through the rainbow from beginning to end, and go into the sky and the universe at the top of the rainbow.

As you're admiring the beauty of the rainbow, you sense the harmony of the colors and decide to take a magical trip through the rainbow to experience and absorb the colors within your body and your mind. You want to feel what the colors are really like. You want to be inside the colors and in tune with the colors, understanding the unique energies and vibrations of each color. Somehow you know that all you have to do is just relax into the rainbow and feel yourself flowing upward through the colors.

Feel yourself rising up into the rainbow, floating gently upward, rising into the color red at the bottom of the rainbow. Feel the color all around you. Breathe in the color and feel it inside you; feel it gently moving through your body. Absorb the color within your mind; feel your mind opening up and becoming more aware as you begin to travel the colors of the rainbow.

Feel yourself rising up into the color orange in the rainbow. Breathing in the color, you become part of the color and the color becomes part of you. Feel it inside you and all around you. Feel it gently vibrating inside your mind. As you absorb the color within your mind, you experience a wonderful feeling of freedom. You feel as if you're standing on the earth and in the sky at the same time.

Feel yourself expanding into the rainbow, rising upward into the color yellow. Breathing in the color, you feel it moving gently within and through your body, within and through your mind. As your mind opens up and becomes more aware, you understand the quality and nature of the rainbow, and you understand the quality and nature of inner truth and knowledge. You feel your inner awareness expanding and increasing as you open up your mind even more.

Flowing into the color green, breathing it inside you, you feel its vibrations resonating in harmony within and through your body and your mind. As you experience it within your mind, you become more in touch with your inner feelings. You feel the color with your emotions, and you're aware that the color nourishes your body as well as your mind. You feel refreshed and healthy as your body and mind experience harmony between themselves.

Expanding your awareness, rising up into the color blue, softly floating and rising higher inside the rainbow, you feel peaceful and tranquil. Breathing in the color, absorbing it within your body and your mind, you feel as if your thoughts are words, and your words are images that spring into action through your feelings. You feel as if you can say and see your thoughts at the same time, and that they're really one and the same, with no difference between the thought and the word. You have a wonderful knowing and understanding that the sky and the earth are really one and the same, with no difference between the universe and you.

As you become aware of this, you rise up into the color indigo inside the rainbow. Breathing in the color of intuitive awareness and spiritual knowing inside you, your mind completely opens up and expands into ever-widening horizons that go far beyond what can be physically seen and touched. You have an understanding and a knowing that goes beyond words and feelings.

As you recognize and accept this awareness within yourself, you enter the color violet at the top of the rainbow. Breathing it inside your body and your mind, and feeling it circulate within you, the color inspires feelings of awe and reverence. You realize that you've opened up your mind's awareness, and you're experiencing your true spiritual nature. You've opened up the spiritual knowing inside your soul, and you understand all that is within you.

If you'd like, you can stay within this rainbow vibration to reflect on what you became aware of and what you felt inside each color of the rainbow. If you'd like to relax a bit more in the rainbow, to deepen your level of relaxation and raise your subconscious/spiritual awareness, stay in the rainbow for a while. Meditate and see what comes to you. If you'd like to stop for a while, use the following script; it will bring you back down to earth. If you want to continue with your past life regression, stay in the color violet at the top of the rainbow. Your past life journey continues in the next chapter.

Inside the color violet at the top of the magical, mystical rainbow in your mind, you feel yourself gradually descending through all the colors you've experienced. Take your time as you feel yourself softly blending into the colors of violet, indigo, blue, green, yellow, orange, and red, remembering all the wonderful things you saw and felt and experienced inside each color.

Now you're standing on the ground again, looking up at the rainbow above you. You notice the sunshine, as it begins to disperse all the clouds. The sun feels pleasantly warm and the sunshine is very bright. As you reflect on what you experienced inside the rainbow as you opened up your mind and your spiritual awareness, you know that you've discovered a special treasure within yourself.

Your body and mind vibrate to the energy levels—the vibrations—within the seven colors of the rainbow. In addition to being a vital part of your past life regression, rising into the rainbow affects and influences both your body and your mind in physical and spiritual ways.

Contained within your body, your endocrine system, are chakras—a Sanskrit word meaning "wheels," which are energy centers or vortexes—that are associated with and connected to each color. The energies of your chakras are in tune with and vibrate in harmony with the energies of the seven colors of the rainbow. To oversimplify their energy expressions, and what you experience in each level of awareness, look at the rainbow as waves of energy, vibrating in a gently moving, increasing rhythm of motion.

The rainbow begins with the color red, which vibrates to physical energies. Its corresponding chakra is located at the base of the spine. The rainbow flows into the color orange, which vibrates to emotional and earthy, grounding energies. Its corresponding chakra is located near the spleen and the reproductive organs. The rainbow continues with the color yellow, which vibrates to mental energies, thoughts, and inner knowing. Its corresponding chakra is located in your solar plexus. The rainbow expands into the color green, which vibrates to growth, love, and healing. Its corresponding chakra is located in the heart region. This is the center point between physical and spiritual energies.

Blue vibrates to astral energies; it expresses communication and creativity. Its corresponding chakra is located in the throat area. Indigo vibrates to etheric energies, to your awareness in a higher spiritual framework of wisdom and understanding. Its corresponding chakra is located slightly above your eyes in the center of your forehead. This is also referred to as your mind's eye, third eye, or psychic sight. The color violet, at the top of the rainbow, vibrates to and resonates with the energies of your soul. It is in harmony with your spiritual awareness. Its corresponding chakra is located at the top of your head. This is also referred to as your crown chakra.

There are many physical and spiritual purposes and reasons for completely feeling, experiencing, and being in the colors of rainbow energies. These vibrations give you access to related aspects of your past life memories, to certain thoughts and images that appear to you as you go into and through the colors. By really feeling and focusing on the images you see and the feelings you experience in each color of the rainbow, you may become aware of certain past life events that are connected with each color.

Sometimes emotions and events are lodged in certain frequencies of energy that can be opened up by centering your attention into that color, and also perhaps into a part of your body where the memory is expressing itself, as in the case of an unexplained ache or pain, or a chronic illness that seems to have no reasonable cause in the present.

When I first began teaching, I had laryngitis every time I walked into class. There was no physical cause for me to lose my voice. It just happened whenever I gave a lecture or conducted a workshop. At first I thought it was just nerves, but during a past life regression I became aware of a lifetime in Egypt where my tongue was cut out for sharing secret knowledge. In this lifetime I was unconsciously reacting to that trauma by losing my voice whenever I taught spiritual knowledge.

When I first went through the rainbow, I began choking as I entered the color blue, which is the color of communication and is associated with the throat chakra. The hypnotist bathed my throat in vibrations of blue and continued the past life regression, where I became aware of the reasons for the persecution and was able to heal the trauma with understanding, forgiveness, and white light. By understanding where my symbolic laryngitis originated, and the reasons for it, I was able to let go of the past life trauma that was lodged in my throat chakra, in the color blue. Now I speak clearly, and no longer experience laryngitis when I teach.

One of my clients experienced back spasms when he entered the color red in the rainbow. He had mentioned in the consultation prior to the regression that he had frequent back pain. He had been to several doctors who had done a series of X-rays. All informed him that there was no physical cause for the pain. But the pain was very real for him. When we focused on the color red, he became aware of a lifetime in which he had been stabbed in the back and had died in excruciating pain. Once he became aware of the past life memory, and resolved the issue surrounding it, he had no further recurrences of back pain.

As you traveled upward through the rainbow, you may have become aware of past life images and feelings in the colors. You may have received gifts in the form of insights or answers, or you might have become aware of past life problems or trauma that could be lodged in certain colors. Your images and feelings provide you with avenues to explore either now or at another time. They give you a focus or a pivot point to further explore and expand your past life memories during the regression, to travel further into them or in another related direction.

Your images and feelings may have also offered you insights into something that may or may not be related to a past life. Perhaps you received an answer to a question or an insight into something that was troubling you, or you may have received direction for something that is occurring in your present life right now that you've been wondering what to do about.

If you'd like to, reenter a meditative frame of mind and go inside the rainbow again to completely explore what you became aware of in certain colors of the rainbow that were especially meaningful for you. Expand upon the scenes, images, and feelings you experienced to see where they lead you.

There are many beneficial ways to use the vibrations of each color for present physical and spiritual purposes. You can wear clothes of a certain color or imagine yourself surrounded with the vibrations of a color to achieve specific things. Simply thinking about the color will bring its vibrations to you. The following is a brief sampling of what the colors represent. Go with your feelings about what the colors feel like to you.

If you're feeling tired or have the blahs, surround yourself with the color red; it will energize you. Red is also the color of passion. Orange expands your instincts and is very earthy; it will ground you and put you in touch with your true feelings in any situation. Yellow enhances your inner knowledge and helps you open up your intuitive nature and the inherent power of your mind. Green promotes healing and harmony, growth and love. Blue relaxes, calms, and soothes you; it takes the edge off bad feelings or experiences. Indigo opens up your psychic perceptions and enhances the mystical power of your mind. Violet helps you become more aware of your true spiritual nature, and is the doorway to the universe within you.

SIDE TRIP . . . THE RAINBOW PATH

Take a more than magical journey through the rainbow to find spiritual gifts and treasures within the vibrations of each color. Go through the rainbow again, not for past life purposes, but to find the gifts that are there. Let yourself completely experience the gifts that are offered. Before you begin, enter a meditative frame of mind.

As you rise into the color red, you see a majestic mountain before you, filled with trees and grassy meadows, gardens and rivers, hills and valleys, plateaus and waterfalls that are touched and highlighted with rainbow colors. You notice that there are rocks and paths that you can follow. Some of the rocks are small, like stepping-stones; others are boulders. You sense the energy of this mountain, the energy of you, and you know that the mountain is very much alive, just like you. It has its own essence and energy, its own reason for being. Explore its energy inside the color red to see what it has to offer you. You may also want to climb a few of the larger rocks to expand your vision of everything that is on the mountain, and to possibly chart a course for a rainbow path you want to follow.

Feeling drawn to the vibrations of the color orange, you realize that you're grounded in the earth, in your physical awareness. Looking around, you see a cave or an opening in the mountainside. It seems to be lit from within; the glowing orange light beckons to you and you decide to enter, to explore the cave to see what is in there. As you enter into the rich deepness of your mind, you become aware of a special gift within the cave, a spiritual gift that will help you in any way you choose in your life right now.

As you exit the cave, you notice the bright yellow sunshine all around you. It feels warm on your skin and you allow the warmth to fill your body, mind, and spirit. As you absorb the sunlight within yourself, you feel it permeating every part of you with a pleasant, gentle warmth. You feel your mind opening up in the light. Looking up at the sun, you notice that the shafts of light are like a god's eye, filtering through a cloud from the heavens.

One beam of light is especially bright and much larger than the others. It is shining brightly, shimmering with energy. It calls to you gently and you decide to see what makes it sparkle. As you walk forward into the light, you see a podium before you, a lectern where perhaps a wise professor or philosopher would give lectures to his students. On the podium, you see a book of knowledge that is open and waiting for you. Walk over to it and look through the book to see what knowledge and spiritual gifts it has to offer you.

Cradling your book of knowledge in your arms, close to your heart, you see a lush, beautiful green garden, a perfect place of peaceful healing, a spiritual sanctuary. You decide to visit this garden, perhaps to read more of the book or just to relax and enjoy the beauty and serenity of nature, to appreciate the flowers that are budding and blooming there. Your heart feels complete joy at being in this beautiful healing place of harmony. As you breathe in the pure, fresh, clean air, and the scent of the greenness and flowers all around you, you feel the air and the greenness revitalizing and rejuvenating you, filling every part of your body, mind, and spirit with health. Enjoy the health that is given to you.

Feeling completely healthy in body, mind, and spirit, you look up at the blue sky above you and see the expansiveness of the universe. The blue seems to go on forever. You feel as if you're in tune with the universe, and you know that you can ascend into the blue, that you can communicate with the sky and that, in turn, the sky will share its secrets with you. You feel yourself being drawn up into the sky, into the universe. As you enter the blueness of the sky, you feel its smooth softness. The blue surrounds you so completely that you feel your essence merging with it, rising up even higher. The blueness of the sky has a soft texture, a feeling of complete peace, a knowing that your soul has traveled this way before. Converse with the sky; listen to what it says to you, hear what it tells you, and see what it shows you and offers you.

As you're traveling through the sky, learning its wisdom, you see a purplish-blue cloud, an indigo cloud, that both excites and scares you at the same time. It excites you because of the unique beauty of its color, and it scares you because it reminds you of a thundercloud and you think that perhaps the storm will let loose at any moment. But then a peaceful feeling comes over you, an intuitive knowingness of the power within the cloud, within you. As you enter the cloud, you see an indigo flower in its center, and you know the past, present, and future of this flower. You see it first as a bud, just beginning to open up, and you realize that it is your spiritual awareness beginning to open up. Watch as the indigo flower continues to open up, as your awareness continues to open up, to bloom and blossom into inner wisdom and knowledge, into the realness of inner knowing and spiritual awareness.

As you're meditating on this beautiful flower, watching it open up, seeing your inner knowing and spiritual awareness open up, you ascend into the color violet at the top of the rainbow above the indigo cloud. You know that the color violet has been formed from indigo blending with the white light of the universe. Within the color violet, you feel special, sacred. You feel an awe and reverence within you, deep within your soul. There is a hushed stillness that is very calming, very peaceful, and you sense something very ethereal in the violet light that is vibrating and pulsating all around you, as if it were alive.

You close your eyes for a moment, to fully absorb the color within yourself, to breathe it in and feel it permeate and fill every part of you. When you open your eyes, you see a beautiful chapel. Perhaps this chapel is on the top of the mountain and was temporarily hidden from view until you raised your awareness into the sky and the universe. Perhaps the chapel is in a clearing inside a forest. Perhaps the chapel is inside your soul. Enter the chapel and see what is within. Your gift is within. Perhaps it is a tangible gift, something that exists in your physical world. Perhaps it is a prayer that has been answered, or a desire that has been granted, or perhaps it is a sense of direction that you know you must follow to travel the rainbow path in your mind.

The things you felt, saw, and experienced on this mystical, majestic mountain in each color of the rainbow, and the gifts that were given to you, were presented to you from the higher part of yourself, from your soul. These gifts were given to you for you to use in your life in any way you desire to make your life better, better, and better.

6

UNIVERSAL LIGHT

W hite light is a universal vibration of energy that has many powerful spiritual applications and practical physical uses. When you enter the white light above the rainbow in the next part of your past life regression, you'll recognize and remember what the light is— the natural vibration of your soul. This is one aspect of white light. You are a being of light; your soul is a divine spark of energy. White light is a powerful source you can draw from within you and from the universe into you, through you, and around you at any time you may want or need it, for any reason and for any positive purpose.

To attune yourself with the energies of white light at any time, simply breathe the pure white light inside you. Breathe it deeply within every part of you, absorbing white light within you, much like how you experience the warmth of sunlight on your skin as it permeates your body. Completely surround yourself with it. Feel it flowing and circulating in, through, and around your body, mind, and soul. Be and become one with the light.

During your past life journey, you'll be surrounding yourself with white light and breathing the pure and positive energies of white light inside you to keep you perfectly safe on physical, emotional, mental, and spiritual levels from feeling any painful or traumatic past life energies, and from bringing negative energies from the past into the present. What you'll bring with you as you return to the present is the understanding of those past life events. You'll be completely aware of the events and emotions, but the energies of the past won't affect you.

To continue with your regression, completely relax your physical body and enter a meditative frame of mind, then go through the rainbow into the color violet at the top of the rainbow. You may experience or feel white light as a mist, as a peaceful, spiritual feeling, as a bright, clear light, or as a shimmering essence. Whatever way you experience it is the way that is most appropriate for you. While white light is very powerful, it is also very peaceful and soothing. As you become energized with white light, the energies will actually relax you as you tune in to your natural spiritual vibrations.

You look above yourself, above the rainbow, and see a shimmering white mist. The light filtering through the mist looks comforting and warm. The mist is a universal white light that is very powerful, pure, and positive in its energy vibration. It sparkles and shimmers with the essence of universal light. The light invites you within and welcomes you; it feels protective and secure, peaceful and spiritual, as you breathe it in and wrap it all around you.

See, sense, and feel yourself in the white mist above the rainbow. It feels peaceful, comforting, and warm. Immerse yourself in it completely. As you enter this shimmering white mist, it feels warm and safe and secure, filled with a quiet power that is both reassuring and spiritually nourishing. You sense and remember how special this light is.

Gathering it all around you and breathing it inside you, you become part of the light, absorbing it within your body, your mind, and your soul. Breathing in the white light of the universe, you know that this white light is also the vibration of your soul. You know that you are truly a powerful spiritual being, and you feel at one with the light and with your soul, in harmony with your spiritual essence.

Breathe in and bring these peaceful vibrations of powerful, spiritual white light energies inside you so that they are vibrating within you and through you, and all around you. As you draw the pure energies of white light within you, you feel it gently balancing and blending your physical and spiritual energies with universal energy as the light cleanses and purifies your body, mind, and soul, as it brings you into harmony with your spiritual awareness, as it keeps you safe and heals you on all levels.

As you bring white light inside you, as the light permeates deep within you, you realize how powerful white light is—how powerful you are—and you simultaneously realize that this same energy resides in a reservoir deep inside you, welling up and releasing the spiritual power you have within you. You sense and feel and know that the essence of your soul is intricately intertwined and interwoven with the universal vibrations of white light, and that your soul is completely in tune with and vibrates to the same peaceful energies as universal light.

Take a few moments to be in the light, to feel the peaceful vibrations, and to experience the harmony of your body, mind, and spirit. Just breathe and be in a natural rhythm and harmony with yourself and white light. You're comfortable and relaxed, peaceful and calm, completely in tune with yourself in a higher level of spiritual awareness and knowing. Breathe white light inside you. Surround yourself with it. Feel it flowing in, through, and all around your body, mind, and soul.

White light will always protect you and keep you safe on your past life journeys as you travel into and through events and emotions you experienced in lifetimes now gone by. You can also use white light to heal any negative past life events, pain, or trauma. White light is always with you; it is always available to you.

Continue to breathe it inside you. It feels like a breath of pure, fresh air that revitalizes and replenishes your energy on every level of your body, mind, and soul. Feel the warmth that flows through your body like a heartbeat, pulsating in a gentle rhythm of protection and safety that feels natural and comfortable as it rejuvenates you with pure and positive energy, as it relaxes and soothes you.

Feel the energy inside you as it circulates through you and surrounds every muscle, every nerve, every bone, every tissue, every organ, every cell, every part of your physical body. As the warmth of white light flows through you, you feel your body gently vibrating and moving in rhythm and harmony with the pure, peaceful, positive energy. It feels natural, normal, and comfortable; you feel completely safe and peaceful, in harmony with your spiritual vibrations.

As you breathe white light inside you, and you accept and absorb it within your mind, you feel your awareness expanding, rising into the vibration of your soul. Breathe white light inside your soul. As you accept and absorb it within your soul, you know that white light will keep you perfectly safe in body, mind, and spirit; it will protect you in all your experiences on your past life journey.

Feel the peaceful, pure, positive vibrations of energy as you breathe in white light, as you surround yourself with it, as you encircle your body, mind, and soul with the white light of physical, emotional, mental, and spiritual protection. Feel white light flowing into you and circulating gently through every part of you. Breathe in the light as you wrap it all around you like a warm and safe aura of knowledge, awareness, and energy. Feel it surrounding you and flowing through you with positive, peaceful energy and protection.

White light is a universal source of energy that is always available to you; it blends with your energy, both within and around you, and keeps you safe on all levels. It's peaceful and powerful at the same time. Feel your increased energy and expanded awareness as you completely encircle yourself with and immerse yourself in white light. Breathe it inside you, feeling it circulate within and through you, wrapping it all around you until you feel absolutely filled and empowered with white light.

After you become familiar with relaxing, rising into, through, and above the rainbow into white light, you can gain access to your subconscious mind and your past life memories by simply breathing in and absorbing white light. You can instantly attain complete physical relaxation and heightened spiritual awareness.

This will be very beneficial in your past life travels. If you are disturbed during your past life regression, you can quickly and easily achieve complete physical relaxation and calmness of mind as you reorient yourself into the place where you left off in your past life regression. Simply breathe in and be one with the light. As you breathe in white light, tell yourself that you will return to whatever you were experiencing in your past life regression.

 SIDETRACKS . . .
Good Vibrations

There are many benefits and positive purposes of white light other than those in connection with past life journeying. There are numerous physical, mental, emotional, and spiritual ways you can use it in every part of your life. In addition to using white light to shield you from and to heal any past life pain or trauma, the energies of white light work wonderfully well for healing your physical body in the present. All you have to do is visualize and feel white light flowing into and through you, within every part of your body, to keep you perfectly healthy. You did this in the healing and harmonizing side trip meditation in Chapter Four.

Using white light for healing is that simple and easy, yet it is also very powerful. Surround yourself with it, breathe it inside every part of you, and bathe in the vibrations of white light. The healing will be effective through your thoughts, feelings, and beliefs about it. If you want to heal a specific ailment, focus and direct white light energies into any part of your body that will benefit from the increased vibrations.

There are many other benefits of using white light for healing your body; it will energize and revitalize you in every way. It will clear all the cobwebs from your mind and remove all the toxins from your thoughts and feelings. It cleanses and purifies you on every level—body, mind, and spirit.

In addition to healing your physical body, there are a multitude of practical and metaphysical applications for white light energy; it works for any positive reason, at any time. The following are only a few uses and suggestions. There are millions of ways to use white light for anything and everything you want to experience and explore, and to help you achieve whatever you want to accomplish.

On a physical level, it can be used for healing, for improving relationships or healing hurtful ones, for helping you to accomplish your goals and your innermost desires, for protecting you in any and all types of situations, for a super shot of energy, for neutralizing every type of negativity, or for changing a negative situation, feeling, or experience into a positive one. You can surround situations, people, places, and things with white light to change the energies and/or enhance them, and to bring about positive results. You can use white light to change your feelings and your attitude. It can turn the blahs into the blissful. You can use white light for anything and everything that you can imagine. The multitude of uses for white light are limited only by your beliefs. The possibilities are endless.

For the purposes of this book, the vibrations of white light are used for protecting you from feeling and reexperiencing any past life pain and trauma, and for healing past life events and emotions. Within the white light, you can remember those experiences and understand why they occurred. It is especially wonderful in helping you to acknowledge and embrace negative feelings, situations, and relationships so that you can understand them, bless them, heal them, and let them go. It allows you to truly forgive and to always come from a loving, white light place within you, within your soul.

White light is your spiritual birthright to use in any way you desire. It always works for the highest good of all. It is also a reminder that you are truly a powerful, spiritual being of light, and that your essence—the light of your soul—shines brightly, radiating and emanating in and through every thought and feeling you have, touching everything you do, and influencing all aspects of every experience you have.

Because white light is a universal light, you can find it every day in the natural energies of sunshine. As you already know, every time you feel the warmth of the sun on your face, it makes you feel good. White light is the reason why. White light is also in lightning and moonlight, though its vibrations are different in each one. Most important, white light is found within you— within your soul. It is your natural vibration of energy.

7

SACRED SPACES

The next step on your past life journey is to be in the sacred space of your spiritual sanctuary. A spiritual sanctuary is a special place of harmony within your heart, mind, and soul where you feel completely at ease, comfortable, safe, peaceful, and perfectly in tune with your spiritual vibrations. It's a sacred space where you're in tune with your soul and in touch with your true spiritual nature. Your sanctuary is a spiritual place that already exists within you. You've been there before in your inner knowing and your spiritual awareness. You've traveled there many times within your soul.

It's a place that waits for you to remember it and to visit it again. It's a place where your soul can reconnect with itself, where it can renew and refresh itself, and where it can rest and reflect. It's a quiet, tranquil place where you enjoy being peaceful, calm, and happy within yourself. It's a place where you're truly in touch with yourself, where you're in tune with the quietness, gentleness, and peaceful vibrations of your inner nature. It's a special, welcoming place where you can be who you really are. It's a magical place where you open up the complete awareness of your mind, where you tune in to your higher self and listen to your inner voice.

It's a sacred space where you reconnect with your true spiritual nature, where you nourish your soul and experience complete harmony within yourself. You may have already rediscovered your spiritual sanctuary in the lush, beautiful garden in the color green inside the rainbow or somewhere else on the rainbow mountain. Your spiritual sanctuary is wherever and whatever you want it to be. Your soul remembers what and where your spiritual sanctuary is, and can return to it for peace and rejuvination.

It can be a place you've been before or a place you remember and create within your mind. Your sanctuary may be symbolic of a feeling you've had or a place you've been where you really felt like yourself and enjoyed being completely at ease. It can represent a mood you've experienced where you truly felt in touch with yourself and in tune with your inner, spiritual nature.

Your spiritual sanctuary may be a beautiful, serene place in the greenness and natural beauty of nature, or it may be somewhere close to the soothing sound of water. It might be a beach, where you listen to the sound of the waves and watch them as they gently ebb and flow. It might be a forest, where you hear the wind gently moving through the leaves in the trees, whispering to you. It might be a wide open expanse of earth, where you view the horizon clearly in all directions. It might be a mountain or a valley. It might be a beautiful lake or a brook with stones that you can walk across. It might be a sparkling stream of water or a wonderful waterfall. It might be a garden or a meadow filled with very beautiful flowers.

It may be reminiscent of a physical place you've been before or it may be a place that you remember from a spiritual memory. It may be a place where you've lived in the interim between lives, where you've experienced your soul in its pure and natural form, or it may be a spiritual place of being-ness or knowing within a multidimensional realm, an energy vibration of pure spirit. It might be a rainbow or it might be the sun. It might be the sky or a cloud. It might be a sunrise or a sunset. It might be the universe or a star. It might simply be the air that you breathe.

Think about or remember the place you'd like to have as your spiritual sanctuary. Your soul will show you what it is and bring you within your sacred space. To continue with your past life regression, reorient yourself into the white light at the top of the rainbow and see, imagine, or remember your spiritual sanctuary.

Within the white light, you become aware of a sacred space—a special place that is your spiritual sanctuary. Take your time to see, feel, imagine, and remember your spiritual sanctuary. Take some time to be there, and to enjoy this very peaceful, sacred place within you.

Go inside the images and feelings that your spiritual sanctuary brings forth and inspires within you; be completely there. See and feel and be in your sanctuary, in this sacred place inside your soul. Look all around and explore your sanctuary to see and know all that is there, and to understand why it is there. Spend some time here to enjoy and appreciate your sacred space. Notice how you feel in your spiritual sanctuary, what you do, and what you think about. Tune in to your feelings; tune in to your soul.

Notice what your spiritual sanctuary looks like. Pay attention to the visual images you become aware of. These images may be symbolic of some of your deep, inner feelings. They may show you scenes from some of your past lives, or offer you the beginning steps into a past life memory. Take some time now—all the time you need—to see all that there is to see in your spiritual sanctuary, and to explore all the things you become aware of. Take some time to enjoy being in this spiritual place within you, within your soul.

Your spiritual sanctuary is an important, valuable part of your past life regression. It's where you both begin and end your past life journey as you reflect on the experiences and emotions you encounter. You can come into your spiritual sanctuary for any reason and at any time during your past life journey, to rest and reflect, to ponder what you are experiencing, to heal past life events and emotions, or just to relax for a while in the healing vibrations of your sanctuary.

Your spiritual sanctuary is where you'll remember and reunite with your higher self, who is the more spiritual part of you, the one who knows all about your experiences in past lives. Your higher self will be your mentor and guide into and through your past life memories. You'll begin your journey here by merging with your higher self, and you'll return to your sanctuary when you're through with your journey before you return to your present, physical reality.

Your spiritual sanctuary is also your safe haven to immediately come to at any time during your past life regression if the memory you are remembering and experiencing becomes traumatic or painful, and you want to remove yourself from the scene for a while, to place yourself in the healing energies of your sacred space. Your higher self will pop you back here the moment you need to be here for any reason, perhaps to remove you from something painful that you're not quite ready to fully experience or to explain the past life trauma you've become aware of in an environment where you feel safe and protected.

This can help you gain more information about the events and emotions you become aware of because your higher self will clearly explain the reason(s) why you need to remember this event and/or emotion and the purpose(s) for it. Your higher self will then take you back into the memory with a much clearer perception and awareness of what is happening, why it is happening, and how it influences and affects your present life.

Your higher self may also bring you back to your spiritual sanctuary to bathe you in white light, to clear and cleanse any negativity, to help you heal the past, and to bring the healing vibrations into the present. You may want to come back to your sanctuary to just take a breather from your past life journey or to reflect on the experiences you've become aware of before you continue into another event, perhaps in a different lifetime, or to raise your vibrations to a higher level to be in tune with the awareness of the memories you'll be experiencing next.

 SIDETRACKS . . .
Present Purposes

There are many wonderful things in and about your spiritual sanctuary that you can enjoy and experience, aside from past life journeying. You can visit this place any time you choose and for any reason. From time to time, you may find gifts and treasures that are left there for you, perhaps from the universe, perhaps from a special angel, or perhaps given to yourself from somewhere inside a dream or another realm of your awareness.

From a practical and purely physical standpoint, your spiritual sanctuary gives you a place to go to at any time to just relax for a few moments, to feel peace and harmony, to refresh and revitalize your body and your mind, and to let go of stress and tension that may build up during your day. It offers you a respite from the physical world and mundane matters. It is also a wonderful place of harmony to be in for a healing of any kind.

Your sanctuary offers you the opportunity to truly get in touch with yourself, to quietly reflect on the things that are happening in your life, to look within yourself to see how and why your experiences originated, and to see the symbology of their spiritual significance. You can find solutions to problems and answers to any questions you pose. Listen to your inner voice, to your true feelings; ask for guidance from your higher self.

Your spiritual sanctuary is so much more than it appears to be. It is a sacred, spiritual place within you that opens up into many wonderful worlds that offer you insight and true understanding into yourself and your soul, worlds that open up into universal knowledge, worlds that show you your spiritual essence. Explore those worlds.

8

YOUR INNER GUIDE

Your inner guide on your past life journey is your higher self, the more aware, knowing part of you, who holds all the information about all the experiences in your past lives—how they happened, why they happened, and the way they affect you now. Your higher self is one aspect of your soul. Who better to guide you on your past life journey than your soul?

Getting in touch with your higher self is very natural; it's tuning in to the spiritual part of you and turning on your spiritual awareness. You may already be aware of your higher self without calling that part of your soul by that term. Way too many people seek spiritual help by looking outside themselves for answers and guidance rather than looking within. They tend to give their power away by searching for outside sources, such as angels, guides, and spiritual masters, who they think must know more than they do about spiritual matters. There's nothing wrong with appealing to these spiritual sources, as they do provide wonderful assistance and insight in times of need.

However, your soul holds all the same information and more than these outside sources can provide you with. Consider this: Maybe all those outside sources you turn to for spiritual sustenance are really various parts of your soul parading in different guises, appearing in the manner you feel most comfortable with. Your soul shows itself to you in this manner to reach you in the way that you're ready to receive and acknowledge those spiritual parts of yourself.

By looking within yourself through a spiritual perception, you're able to see and recognize aspects of your higher self in the various roles your higher self plays in your life. Your higher self is your dream mentor and your spiritual guide into multidimensional realms of awareness and knowing that lead you straight into your soul. Your spiritual guide may also appear as a shamanic power animal—an ally. Your higher self appears as an answer that you've been desperately searching for, speaking to you through your inner voice, an insight that sparkles in your mind, a soothing touch on your shoulder when you most need it, a whisper of love and joy in your heart when you feel utterly sad and despairing.

Knowing your higher self is the most wonderful thing you could ever imagine and then some. Your higher self loves you completely and unconditionally. Your higher self is your spirit-self, the essence of your soul, the spark of light that shines brightly within you. Your higher self is like a whisper of wind that gently surrounds you and caresses you softly as it blows through you, refreshing you with a gentle quiet, a peaceful sense of serenity and harmony, a feeling of joy and wonder. Your higher self is everything that is good and wonderful and warm about you.

Your higher self is, in every sense of the word, your guardian angel, the caretaker of your heart, mind, and soul while you are in physical form. Your higher self is the higher aspect of yourself.

Your higher self is the essence of your soul, the immortal flame of your spiritual existence. Your higher self is what survives after the physical body dies. Your higher self is embodied within your soul.

All of this sounds too wonderful to be true, but it really is true. Your higher self is all that and much more. Believe it because it's true. Look into your heart and mind, and you'll know it's true. Listen to your innermost thoughts and feelings, and you'll hear the truth. Your higher self will whisper to you through your heart and touch you through your soul.

Before you continue reading about your higher self, take a few minutes to think about who your higher self really is, what your higher self has to offer you, and the many ways your higher self has appeared to you at various times in your life. Think about the times you've been in touch with your higher self and how you connected with that part of your soul. After meditating on this for a while, what is your perception of your higher self?

You can perceive your higher self in many different ways. Each one of us becomes aware of our higher self in a way that is unique to us. Some people sense their higher self as an energy or a feeling, sometimes as a glowing light or as a form of light-energy, while others see their higher self as an image of themselves that is knowledgeable and wise in every respect. Some higher selves appear in a symbolic manner as angels, or wise old men, or ancient philosophers or teachers, and some show themselves as a mother or father figure who is nurturing, caring, and comforting. Some higher selves appear as your best buddy.

Some people envision their higher self as a spiritual guide, an entity who is separate from them, outside of them, or above them. Your higher self isn't above you, outside of you, or separate from you in any way; your higher self is an integral part of you. Your higher self is a very special, very spiritual part of you that is always with you in every moment of every lifetime. Your higher self encompasses every part of your soul, and is within every thought you have, every emotion you feel, every experience you have, every action you take, and in all your hopes, dreams, wishes, and desires. Your higher self is within every breath you take and in every heartbeat.

Reuniting with your higher self—with the higher aspect of yourself—is like being with your oldest, dearest, and most trusted friend. It feels like coming home after a long journey in which you were lost, hungry, afraid, and alone, then being welcomed and embraced by the gentleness and love of your spiritual self. If you've been out of touch with your higher self, the reunion is sometimes emotional, filled with a joy and happiness that words cannot describe. To continue with your past life journey, be in the white light above the rainbow and go into your spiritual sanctuary.

In your spiritual sanctuary, you feel in touch with yourself and in tune with your true spiritual nature. You feel very peaceful and quiet, and you feel a heightened sense of awareness and anticipation building inside you. There is a special atmosphere in your sanctuary that you hadn't noticed before, or perhaps you were aware of it but didn't know quite what it was, or maybe you recognized the spiritual vibrations immediately. You sense a special presence that has come into your spiritual sanctuary, and you welcome this awareness that is opening up within you. You know that it is your higher self, the highest aspect of yourself who has come to you. You know that it is your soul, ready to appear to you.

Looking around your sanctuary, you see that your higher self is there, waiting for you. You know that your higher self has always been there, waiting for you to recognize and remember him or her, and that your higher self will always be there. As you look at your higher self, you experience an incredible feeling of respect and trust, love and joy that words cannot describe. The feelings are coming from you and from your higher self at the same time. Take a few moments now to become more aware of your higher self and to enjoy the anticipation of fully remembering all those most special and spiritual parts of yourself.

As your higher self begins to walk toward you, you feel the positive, loving, spiritual feelings that emanate from your higher self, and you sense the energy and knowledge that radiates from deep within your higher self, from deep within yourself, deep within your soul. As you move forward to reunite with your higher self, with the spiritual part of you, you experience a wonderful feeling of joy and happiness. As your higher self embraces you, you feel yourself merging into knowledge, awareness, and light. You know that you've found the higher aspect of yourself; you've come home to yourself, and you've embraced your soul. In your own way, and in the manner that feels most right for you, become more in tune with your higher self, with your soul. Feel the rapport you have with your higher self that strengthens the bond between you as you more fully open up your spiritual knowledge and awareness.

When you're done, breathe deeply for a few moments, feeling the harmony within yourself, feeling the harmony you have with your higher self. Breathe in the awareness and understanding of everything you've rediscovered and remembered about your higher self, about your soul. Reflect on what you experienced as you reunited with your higher self. Ponder all your feelings and thoughts about your higher self. Reflect on how your higher self appeared to you and how you responded to your higher self. Remember what your higher self said to you and what your higher self did. This helps you become even more aware of your higher self and all the knowledge you have within your soul. Knowing your higher self is a prelude to becoming aware of all the various parts of your soul and understanding your true spiritual nature.

THE ROLE OF YOUR INNER GUIDE

Your higher self is your inner guide and will lead you, with understanding and insight, into and through your past life journey and will clearly explain everything you experience. While you may have some preconceived ideas about the experiences in the past life you'll be exploring, based on what is happening in your present life right now or the past life you want to explore, don't be surprised if your higher self shows you something entirely different. Let go of any preconceived notions that might restrict or interfere with your past life journey.

Your higher self is your intuitive and very knowledgeable guide who will show you what you most need to see, know, and experience at this time. During your past life regression, always, always, always—I cannot emphasize or stress this enough—*always* follow the guidance of your higher self. Your higher self has your best interests at heart and will guide you with great care and understanding into and through your past life memories.

Your higher self will guide you through everything you're seeing and experiencing. Talk to your higher self. Ask questions. Ask for clarity. Ask why you're being shown the events you are seeing and experiencing. Your higher self will explain everything that is occurring to you, and what you are feeling and why you are feeling it, during your past life journey to help you perfectly understand what is happening and why it is happening. Your higher self will show you the purpose for it in the past and its relevance to your present life by clearly explaining how the past experience relates to your present life, to give you greater insight and understanding. If your higher self is silent for a while, it is because you already know the answers within and can find the understanding within yourself.

Before you begin your past life journey, while you're in your spiritual sanctuary, you can ask your higher self for ways to resolve a present problem that may have its origins in a past life. Your higher self will guide you into the relevant past life and show you how to reconnect with the past life experience in order to understand and resolve the problem, and to see its spiritual significance in your present life.

Your higher self will explain who the current people in your life were in past lives and your relationship with them in the past. Your higher self will show you the karma that was incurred between you and explain the reasons for being together with them again. Your higher self will help you understand all the aspects of your karma and guide you through the balancing and healing process. Your higher self will show you how and help you to heal any negative past life pain or trauma.

Trust your higher self; trust your inner knowing. Accept what you see and become aware of in the way that it is shown and offered to you, and experienced by you. All the things you want to know and become aware of, and have explained to you, will occur very naturally in their own appropriate time, sequence, and flow. Don't allow your conscious thoughts to intrude or interfere. If you find that you are resisting an experience, or you are trying to consciously direct your past life journey to where you think it should go or where you want it to go, or you're struggling for details or an answer that doesn't come right away, just let it go. Listen to your higher self.

SIDETRACKS . . .
Present Purposes

You may already know your higher self as your inner self, or as the little voice that whispers to you from the quietness of your mind through your thoughts, dreams, and feelings. You may hear your inner voice in a meditation or when you are in certain situations. Your inner voice is sometimes referred to as hunches, intuition, or a sense of just knowing something. Your inner self is part of your higher self.

Your higher self is within every part of your life, from the mundane to the magical. Be in touch with your higher self, with the higher part of yourself, every day in your thoughts. Simply be quiet and meditate to open up your spiritual awareness. Listen to your higher self through your feelings. Your higher self is aware of everything about you, and offers you direction and guidance in your life on both a physical and a spiritual level.

You can give all your problems and worries to your higher self. Your higher self will handle them with understanding and knowledge, and will show you the best, most loving way to take care of them. You can go to your higher self for any reason; your higher self will accept whatever you're feeling and experiencing, and will show you how to understand yourself in a better and clearer way.

Your higher self does so much more than guide you on past life journeys. Touching the essence of your higher self is magical and mystical. Your higher self plays a vital role in every part of your life. You can bring your higher self awareness into all your everyday experiences. Simply act in, through, and from the energy of your higher self in every moment of every day, in all your thoughts and activities. Listen to your feelings and follow your heart.

PART III

KARMIC CONNECTIONS

Past/Present People in Your Life

There are people in your present life whom you've known before in your past lives. Perhaps you've met someone for the first time and felt an instant familiarity with him or her, or there was a soul recognition somewhere inside you. Maybe you felt a closeness and a sense of comfort with a certain person right away, as if he or she were a long-lost friend and you were picking up exactly where you had left off. Friends, lovers, and special family members you've known and shared previous lives with are kindred spirits.

They're in your present life in a variety of relationships. Your mother now may have been your sister or a favorite aunt in a past life. Your brother may have been your best friend or your daughter. Your father may have been your boss or your son in a past life. Your sister may have been your grandfather. The combination of ways that you are connected with past souls, and the relationships you share with them, vary from lifetime to lifetime, though sometimes you are in the same relationships. This is most often true of husband and wife duos, though you may switch sexes. This is because of the special love your soul has for that person.

Your enemies from the past are also in the present. Look at the people you currently have problems with and you may recognize them as past life people who have shown up in your present to give you a hard time. But then again, maybe they're special souls who have come into your present life to help you learn a lesson or to balance some bad karma between you so that you can both grow from the experience and evolve your souls.

Both your past life friends and your past life enemies are easy to recognize because of the feelings you have about them now and the situations you're involved in with them. The present reflects what occurred in the past. Look within your present relationships and inside your feelings to become aware of the similarities to past life relationships and dramas, and you'll see the karmic connection you have with other souls.

For example, let's say you have a problem with your boss. He's always pushing you to get your work done on time and makes you repeat what you've already done because he says that it's not good enough. Maybe you have a feeling that he was your domineering father in a past life and wasn't accepting of you because nothing you did was ever good enough. You were always trying to please him, even though you knew that what you did was the best you could do. In the process you began to lose your belief in yourself and you bought into this other person's belief that you weren't good enough. This is the karma that you've carried over—a tendency to be a people pleaser rather than to please yourself. This same soul is in your present life for several possible reasons, maybe so you can resolve the karmic conflict by accepting yourself and learning how to stand up for yourself.

Another possible variant is that this soul pushes you to be better because he wants to help you grow your soul or maybe because he's just a mean, nasty tyrant and likes to put people down. Maybe you were a mean, nasty tyrant in one of your past lives and your karma now is to experience what that feels like—to experience what you've done to other people. Or maybe you bent over backwards to please this other person and you let him walk all over you.

For whatever reason, the karmic situation is in your life so you can grow your soul. The karmic test is how you respond to the situation now by either creating more bad karma or dealing with it in a positive manner. If you resolve the situation—through your feelings in the relationship and by taking appropriate action—the karma is balanced. If you don't resolve the situation, you carry over the karma into another lifetime or later in this life where a similar situation will arise again.

Perhaps you have problems with your teenage daughter. While rebelliousness is a characteristic of adolescents, there may be past life problems tied in with the present. One of my clients had a running conflict with her runaway daughter. She loved her daughter, but they couldn't get along. In a past life regression, she became aware of a past life in which she abandoned her fourteen-year-old daughter. Now her daughter was trying to abandon her. The mother's karma was a payback for what she had done as well as a test to see if she would abandon her daughter again, and the situation was also in her life to help her learn how to resolve the emotions of fear and rejection that she put on her daughter in a past life by experiencing it herself. Her daughter is in her life in this similar situation to resolve her feelings of abandonment, and also to help her mother deal, in a loving way, with the feelings of guilt and remorse that she had as a result of abandoning her daughter in a past life.

If you're continually involved in rotten relationships that follow a similar course, or you're always getting dumped on, you could have been a rather nasty person in one or more of your past lives. What you're experiencing now in your relationships is what you did to others in the past. Your karma is to experience the hurtful feelings that you caused other people, and to resolve and heal those feelings to grow your soul. Or maybe you're involved in bad relationships because you want to learn inner qualities of love and acceptance to advance your soul.

The theme of cheating on one's spouse is a common scenario in past life and present relationships. The karma is usually a turn-around. If you cheated on your spouse, you'll probably be cheated on this time around, though that's not always necessarily true. If your spouse is cheating, the karma is usually to learn how to deal with those feelings in a positive, loving manner. Many times, your cheating spouse is a special soul who is in your life in this type of relationship to help you deal with it in a positive manner and to return both your souls to the love you have deep within you. Another reason for cheating spouses is that this soul isn't right for you, but is in your life as a friend to help you become a more loving person. Difficult relationships are always in your life for a positive purpose.

Your karma, whether good or bad, is interwoven with the relationships and experiences you have with people in your life. The energies of events that have occurred and the emotions contained within relationships are not affected by time. Your soul carries over the past energies of experiences into the present to continue something you began before that needs to be completed because the karma wasn't balanced in the past or to continue something that was good and filled with love.

You also carry over past energies to learn soul lessons, or bring something from the past into the present that can now be enhanced. Love carries over very strongly; the love you feel for certain people from past lives reappears in the present. The past shows up in the present in similar feelings, situations, and relationships.

Once the energies of past emotions arrive in the present, they are further expanded and perpetrated, playing out within the present interactions between you and the soul you're karmically connected to. You choose to be with people you've known before in various relationships to provide you with opportunities to balance karma or to just enjoy being with them again. When you meet them in this life, your soul remembers them. Your soul remembers the events you've experienced and the emotions you've shared with them in the past.

Becoming aware of people from the past who are in the present helps you understand the relationship you shared before and the reasons you have the experiences now that you have with them. Remembering and recognizing previous souls helps you to know what needs to be done to balance the karma between you. You may already have a feeling—either vague or an absolute certainty—that some of your friends and enemies were with you before. During your past life regression, you'll become aware of the roles they played then. You'll see how the interactions between you in the past have influenced the roles you both play now, the reasons why you both engage in the situations you experience, and why you have the feelings that you do now.

People you're karmically connected to are in your life to either enhance the relationship you've shared before or to balance the karma that was created in the past. Quite often, the relationship is a combination of both. The karma you share with people in your life surfaces in many different ways. When you look at the situations and how you feel about them, when you understand what you have experienced in your relationships and let your thoughts flow along the lines of how the present mirrors the past, you can become aware of the past life tie that connects you with a certain person or persons. The reason you're with certain people at this time in your life is to either continue the love you feel for this soul or because the circumstances are right for balancing your shared karma.

As you work with the information you receive during your past life regression, you'll discover the how and why of the karma that needs to be balanced with another person. You'll know why your soul chose to experience the karmic situation in the manner that it appears in this lifetime, and what your soul hopes to learn from it. Many times, people will request a past life regression because of problems in their relationships. Before they come in for the session, they've usually got a good handle on what needs to be corrected and what caused it in this life, and how a past life may be partly to blame for present difficulties.

During the regression, you'll remember and become clearer on past life issues you've carried over that are mirrored in present problems, as your higher self guides you into the lifetime where the problem began with this person, and shows you lifetimes where the negativity was continued and perpetuated. Your higher self will give you insight and understanding into how and why this problem began in a past life, tell you why you're experiencing it now, and what you need to learn from having this experience. Listen to what your higher self says. It is your inner knowing, your soul awareness, speaking to you.

SIDE TRIP . . . RESOLVING RELATIONSHIPS

When you have problems in a present relationship with past life people, it's always helpful to completely understand the problem, and all the parts and pieces of the past life influences on it, before you balance the karma that is shared between you. Understanding it allows you to see how and why it originated, and shows you the various parts you both played in the origin and continuation of negative events and emotions, and the reasons you've carried it over into the present. It provides you with a complete picture so you can cleanse all the negativity.

Viewing your current relationship from an in-depth, honest perspective will give you answers and insight into both yourself and the other person, and the relationship you have. It will help you open up even more information in your regression while it shows you the origins of the problem and the resulting karma to be balanced with this person. This gives you insights into the present problems you have and your responses to the relationship, and helps you see how the past and present problems are intertwined and perpetuated.

Think about someone in your life with whom you're experiencing problems. Think about the problem you're experiencing with this person and how it began in this life. Consider your attitude toward, and your emotions about, this person and the problem. What do you feel the karma is that you need to balance with him or her? Why do you think he or she is in your life? Just let the answers flow into your mind.

This information will come through in great detail in the past life regression, but you can get a head start by gathering information that will be expanded upon and enhanced as you revisit the past events that are connected with this person. Before you begin this side trip, enter a meditative frame of mind and surround yourself in an aura of loving white light.

To delve deeper into the present relationship and the past life experiences you both shared, picture this person in your mind and think about your feelings for him or her. Your feelings will connect you with the past life memory. Just let your thoughts flow into the experiences in a past life that you shared with this individual. Perhaps you'll see scenes, or you may become aware of feelings, or you'll have a sense about where you are and what you're doing or what is happening.

When you're there in the past life experience, see what is happening and look at the part you both had in creating the shared karma. You may either feel the scene or be in the scene. Be with this experience for a while, and then go above the scene into your soul awareness. From this expanded level of awareness, your higher self will help you understand how your past emotions and attitudes color the feelings you have about the person now and the shared problem. This helps you separate the past from the present and puts you in touch with your true feelings. It will show you all the various past and present parts of your experiences with this person.

See the origins of the past negativity that is now showing itself in the present. Watch the past and present energies to see how they interweave through time in your relationship, and to understand why you've carried this past experience over, why you chose to have this experience in your present life. Clearly see how and why the problem began to understand what your soul desires to learn from it. See how the problem was carried over from the past. See the part you played in it. Look for negative decisions and choices you've made on a soul level in the past about this relationship. See how those previous decisions and choices, coupled with intense emotional feelings, were carried over from the past life experience and are reflected in what you're experiencing now.

The past situation is not the only precipitating agent for the present problem. To become aware of the agreements your souls both made to one another before birth into this lifetime regarding this karma, your higher self will guide you into the interim between lives when you were preparing for this life and making decisions and choices with this person. Your higher self will provide you with the awareness and understanding of the soul agreements and promises you made to each other, and to the experiences you both agreed to have in order to balance the shared karma and learn soul lessons. Immerse yourself in the expanded awareness you have within this spiritual realm— the awareness that you had when you were choosing and creating the current circumstances that you agreed to share with this person—the circumstances that would enable you to resolve the problem and heal the relationship.

The insights your higher self gave you and the information you've gathered from looking into the past and into your true feelings in the present will help you understand your current relationship better, to see its origins in past life events, and how your soul desires to resolve the difficulty. This information gives you answers and helps you to understand what you're experiencing now and why you're experiencing it. It also helps you understand why you've co-created and are participating in the present problem. It allows you to see all the parts of the shared experiences.

To become aware of how to best resolve the problem in the present, and to balance the shared karma from the past, your higher self will show you many loving ways to take care of the problem and to balance your karma in the process in a positive way. This is something you'll also be doing in the past life regression. Perhaps all you need to do is to accept what happened without placing any blame or holding any regrets, forgive the other person and/or yourself, bless the situation(s) or experience(s) and let it go, then surround it with white light to heal it. Or perhaps some positive action in the present is required to resolve the difficulties.

All the insights and information you became aware of in this meditative journey of knowing build the background for understanding and resolving karma with all the people in your life. You can use this knowing to help you heal your past life relationships, to make them all better in the present, and to evolve your soul.

 SIDETRACKS . . .
Present Purposes

While it's important to understand, balance, and heal hurtful past life relationships, it's just as important, maybe more important, to heal present life relationships before they turn into future life relationships with bad karma attached to them. Healing brings you inner peace, harmony, and happiness, not to mention resolving all those nasty, negative energies so you can let them go, rather than carrying them around and continuing to let them hurt you.

By taking care of people problems in the present in a positive, loving manner, you eliminate the need for bad karma to carry over and continue from the past or to surface in the future from the present. By resolving present issues and conflicts in relationships, you're either balancing the bad karma from the past or creating good karma that you'll experience later in this life or in another life.

A good way to heal any hurt you may be feeling, and to resolve any existing problems you may have in a relationship, is to simply accept what is happening in the present for what it is, without any feelings of anger, judgments, blame, regrets, desire for revenge, or any further perpetration of negativity. Know that this situation is in your life to help you grow and learn, to bring you peace and harmony, and that you chose to have this experience to help you evolve your soul. Focus on all the positives within the negative. Be thankful for this experience, whatever it may be. See what you've gained from it—how it has made you a better person and helped you to evolve your soul—forgive yourself and/or the other person for the part each of you played, and then simply let it go.

Don't hold on to any of the hurt, don't place blame anywhere, and don't entertain regrets. You're only free of it if you completely let it go in a positive, loving manner. During the regression, you'll have an increased understanding of why certain problems are happening in a relationship, and you'll be able to bless those experiences for what they have shown you about your soul and how they have helped you to grow spiritually.

You'll be able to heal past life events and emotions that have hurt you and other souls, perhaps using white light, and to let them go with love. You'll be able to come from a loving, white light place in your soul. Love is when everything is in balance; it's the natural vibration of your soul. Speaking of love, the following meditations will show you the power of love to heal anything, whether it occurred in the past or the present, to bring more love into your life, and to meet your soulmate, if you haven't already met him or her.

SIDE TRIP . . . A LOVE MEDITATION FOR YOUR HEART AND SOUL

Today, right now, is a day of love. It is a day for enhancing relationships, rekindling feelings, letting love into your heart, and opening up your soul to expand the love. It's a day for bringing love into your life or for strengthening the love you have. It's a day for forgiving past hurts and freeing yourself to move forward. It's a day for healing any hurts in your heart. It's a special day for all kinds of love—romantic love, parent-child love, special friendship love—and most especially, it is a day of loving yourself. Love begins within, then expands outward to encircle everyone in your life with love. As you send the love out that is within you, the love that is within your heart and soul, it resonates with and radiates energy and returns to you many times over. Today is the day to love others, to love their souls. Today is the day to love yourself, to feel the love within you, within your soul.

Feel totally, completely, unconditionally loved. Let this feeling fill you until you are overflowing with it, until your heart is completely filled with the joy and happiness and feeling of it. Love surrounds you so completely, and totally immerses you within its vibration, that you and love are one and the same. Love is in the air. Breathe it in. Breathe it out. Breathe it inside you; feel it circulating within and through you, opening up your heart, freeing you from any and all past hurts, letting them go in an easy, carefree, loving manner. You feel so filled with the blessings and bliss of love that there is room for nothing else. Pure, powerful, wonderful, joyful love courses through your entire being.

Feel this love permeating every part of your life—past, present, and future. Feel it radiating out from you to everyone in your life.

Feel it surrounding you in every situation, in every relationship, and in every experience. The more love you give, the more love there is to give. The more love you give, the more love there is to receive. See everything totally filled with love and surrounded by love. See and feel every part of your physical body completely encircled and embraced with love, inside and out. See and feel your mind growing and expanding into love, letting the light of love shine in all your thoughts.

See and feel your heart totally filled with pure abundant love—a special, soulful love that radiates and emanates through every part of you, flowing within and from you, like a rhythmic, pulsating heartbeat, like the breath of life in a dance of harmony with all that is around you and within you. Breathe it in, breathe it out in a joyful sharing. See and feel every part of your entire existence filled with this beautiful, wonderful, magical, powerful, mystical energy vibration of love.

See and feel your heart and soul completely immersed in love. Share this love with yourself, with every thought in your mind, with every emotion in your heart, and within every experience your soul has ever had. Share this love with everyone you know. Surround them all in this vibration of love that courses through your being and radiates from your heart, mind, and soul.

This meditation completely opens your heart to love, and allows you to let go of any and all hurts, whether they happened in the past or the present. It fills you completely with so much joy and happiness that it will spill over into every part of your life, touching everyone you know and everything you do. It will also begin to open up the space for your soulmate to come into your life.

SIDE TRIP . . . MEETING YOUR SOULMATE; DRAWING HIM OR HER TO YOU

Have you ever met someone for the first time and felt very strongly that you knew him or her before? Maybe you felt a close companionship, a connection, a rapport, a familiarity with him or her. Perhaps you had an absolute knowing that this person was a special and very dear friend from long ago, from another lifetime.

Maybe you felt a rush of excitement or a heat wave of love flow through you. Perhaps your heart skipped a beat or it was pounding with recognition and remembered love. Maybe there was a knowing look in this person's eyes that were mirrored in yours. Perhaps you puzzled over where you met this person before, but your soul knew the truth. Your soul recognized your dearly beloved soulmate.

If you've already met your soulmate, you've experienced all the above and then some. It's like a lightning bolt that hits you as love courses through your entire being. Your heart remembers and your soul knows the joy. If you haven't yet met your soulmate in this lifetime, the following meditation will open up the energy vibrations and the space for this very special person to come into your life.

Love is in the air. You feel it all around you as you breathe it deeply within yourself, feeling it flow softly and gently through you, through your soul. Your heart is totally open, ready, and waiting for love to pour in; ready and waiting, eager to experience the pure and powerful love of your soulmate, the one who is the other part of your soul, the other part of you. The one who holds the key to your heart, the one you desire to share all your love with completely—in body, mind, heart, and soul.

Your heart yearns for the love of your remembered soulmate. You yearn to share your special love with your soulmate. You desire to share your life with your soulmate, to share many moments, many months, and many years of happiness and joy together. You know that the moments, even the mundane ones, are magical because you share them with someone special, with the love of your life who lights up your eyes, warms your heart, and touches your soul.

You know that your soulmate is close, perhaps not physically at the moment, but emotionally you are already one soul that is joined, not two separate souls searching for one another. Maybe your soulmate is only a moment away, a breath away, a heartbeat away. You feel a breathless anticipation, waiting for your soulmate to appear in your life. As you take a deep breath in and surround your heart and soul with love, you feel the energies around you change. The vibration is quickened, like a pulse of life, like a heart-beat, like a wave of love.

You can feel your soulmate touching your soul from long ago and far away, reaching through time to meet you again in this lifetime, to share the love that your souls have shared for centuries, for eons of time, since the beginning of time. In your mind's eye, in your soul's heart, you see and remember both of you walking together in a warm sunrise, holding hands, feeling your hearts entwined for all of past, present, and future eternity. You feel the memory of all the times and all the love you've shared with one another.

These feelings of connection, these remembrances of your heart and soul, bring forth a deep, bubbling, wonderful joy that surfaces and races through your heart, as you rekindle and reawaken in your soul the love you share with this person, as you experience a timeless reconnection, a joyful reunion. You know that even though your bodies are in different forms now, and you have other names, you recognize the glow, the aura, the soul-essence that your souls share. Bathe in the warm, loving glow that's been rekindled between your souls. You know, within your soul, that you are holding hands and touching hearts across dimensions of time and space, renewing your love and watching it grow.

Release your feelings, your desires to have your soulmate in your life, into the air around you. Whisper your wishes to the wind and let it blow to the corners of the earth, to the farthest reaches of the universe, whispering to your soulmate's heart. The wind knows where your soulmate is. Make your request from all the love that is within your heart. Send your message, your desire to be with your soulmate again in this lifetime, out into the world to find your soulmate, and to guide him or her to you on the breath of love and the light wings of air. Tell the universe, tell the higher power of your soul, to direct your soulmate to you. Your soulmate's heart hears and will respond. Know that your soulmate will appear in your life when the time is right for your souls to be together and to share your love again.

Love is the natural vibration of your soul. It is the core of your soul's existence. Love is always the answer, always the way to balance and heal past life problems with present life people.

10

KARMA

What is karma and what does it mean to you in the context of day-to-day living? Karma means action and is energy in motion. There's good karma and there's bad karma. Karma is the replaying of the energies of events that you set in motion in your past lives through your thoughts, feelings, actions, and responses to the situations, relationships, and experiences you were involved in. Good karma gets even better; bad karma strives for balance, to make wrong things right.

The karma you originated, and participated in, in past lives shows up in the present. Bad karma is the replaying of past life experiences in which you did or reacted to something in a negative way. When it reappears in a similar situation in the present, you are given the opportunity to correct it. Karma can best be described as what goes around, comes around. For all intents and purposes, karma is cause and effect. An event or emotion in a past life is the cause that creates the effect that you experience in your present life.

You created the manner in which your karma shows itself in your present life. Karma isn't something that pops out at you from somewhere in your past. Your soul is fully aware of what you chose to experience and how you chose to experience it. You chose the experiences you would have in this lifetime to help you evolve your soul. This is important to keep in mind. You're responsible for everything you experience in your present life, even if you don't remember consciously creating it or choosing to experience it.

Your actions from past lives repeat themselves in similar experiences in your present life. These similar situations occur when the energies of your past and present experiences intersect. They happen when something in your present life is similar to what occurred in one or more of your past lives. Karma works the way that it does by coming full circle in the present and offering you the opportunity to balance. Karmic situations, relationships, and dramas will repeat themselves in different versions until you get it right, until you correct what is wrong, thereby bringing the past and present energies into balance.

The nature of karma strives for balance. Karma is a good thing; it shows you that you are striving to right past wrongs. It works the way that it does to help you evolve your soul. Knowing what your karma is and deciding what you want to do about it is an important part of your past life regression. As you become aware of who you were before, what you did in your past lives, what happened to you, and why you acted and reacted the way that you did, you'll see how and why your past experiences repeat themselves in the present; you'll understand how and why they affect you now. You'll understand why you chose to experience your karma in the way that you do in this lifetime. Your karma surfaces when a present situation or emotion reflects past life actions, when the past energies intersect with present energies and are put into motion.

You don't even have to look for your past in the present; your past will find you. You don't have to remember what you created for yourself to experience in this lifetime to learn soul lessons and to balance your karma. Your current situations and experiences will show you what your karma is. The similarities between your past and present situations is the karmic connection. You tune in to and get in touch with karmic energies through your emotions, through your feelings of why certain situations are happening to you.

Your emotions pull the past life memory up to the surface and out into the open because the energy of your emotions are very powerful and are intricately intertwined with your memories. You may not consciously remember your past life experiences, but somewhere inside you, you do remember the emotions associated with them and contained within them. Your emotions transcend time; they continue from lifetime to lifetime. You can see how the past is reflected in the present; you can sense and feel the energy of past events and emotions by focusing on what is happening in the present and how you're feeling about it to lead you into the vibes from the past.

Your emotions, in both the past and in the present, are very powerful. They surface easily and will show you what your karma is, without any holding back. While you may have forgotten negative events that you experienced in past lives, your feelings always remember. Your feelings are a direct link to the karmic events that occurred, and will show you the significant events in your past lives. During your regression, pay attention to your feelings. They'll help you get to the underlying cause of past life events and will be a key factor in helping you to balance and heal those events.

Past life memories surface when something—a situation, a relationship, or an experience—in your present life is similar to something that occurred in a past life. They show up because the energies of certain circumstances are right for balancing. This occurs through the karmic connection, when a present situation or feeling resonates with a similar past life experience in which those same events and/or emotions were experienced. You can get a good handle on what your karma is from the past by looking into your present experiences that are giving you problems or are not going the way you want them to.

You can also see what your karma is by looking into all the good things and positive experiences you have in your life. Many people mistakenly think of karma as always being bad. Karma can be good or bad, depending on what you've done and how you've reacted to the people, events, and emotions in your past lives. The past can come back in the present to help or haunt you. Experiences and emotions carry over from lifetime to lifetime; they're connected through your experiences and feelings to let you enjoy what you've done or until they're understood and resolved.

Before you look at your bad karma, look at all the good karma you've created and experienced in your past lives, which you've carried over into your present life. While it's important to balance negative karma, it's also very important to enjoy the rewards of good karma that you've racked up. Good karma surfaces in many ways in the present. Perhaps you're involved in a wonderful, loving relationship with your soulmate, or you have friends and family that you feel very connected with. Your closeness with these people was begun in previous lives and carried over and continued through one or more past lives.

If you're very successful in your career and feel that it's your calling, it was probably begun in a previous life and you've carried over your skills into this life. If everything comes easily to you now, you probably struggled for it in the past; the present is the payoff for all your hard work. Look at all the good you have in your life and you'll see the rewards you've earned. This is your good karma and it only gets better from here.

Karma isn't something that just happens to you. You're not stuck with negative karma if you don't want to be stuck with it. Before you were born into this life, you chose the experiences you would have in your present life. You chose the karma to carry over. You welcomed it with open arms to give yourself the opportunity to balance your previous actions and to evolve your soul. But you can always change your mind. You don't have to deal with karma if you don't want to, but here's another *but,* and this is a big *but.* If you don't deal with it now, when it shows up in your life, you will deal with it later in this life or in a future life. There's no getting away from it. Your soul wants to balance your karma, even if you'd rather walk away from it.

Within the realm of reincarnation, you always have free will. You're not locked into anything because you can always change your mind. That's what free will is all about. Karma isn't something that happens to you that you have no control over. Your experiences are the karma you chose to have showing up in the present. When you see your karma playing itself out in a present situation, you may feel at first that you can't do anything to change it. Wrong. This is where your free will comes in. You always have free will to make choices and changes about every situation in your life, whether those situations originated in your past lives or you created them in the present as part of the reality you want to experience.

It's easy to see what your karma is showing you and what it is saying about your soul and why you chose to experience it. You can see what your karma is and know how to correct it by looking at what you're currently experiencing. If you're dealing with negative issues, look at the positive side of them. This will give you big clues. The key is to look at the opposite of what's happening. For example, if you're deaf, maybe you didn't listen to others in a past life and not being able to hear is your karma. To balance your karma, you need to learn how to listen in a symbolic manner.

While this sounds simplistic, look deeper. Perhaps you didn't listen to yourself in the past, so your karma could be to listen to yourself, to value your feelings and opinions. Perhaps in the past, your right to say what you felt was squelched and rather than speak up, you settled for silence. Now silence is what you hear. By not speaking up when you knew that you should, your silence caused someone harm.

Or perhaps you were constantly running off at the mouth and people got tired of listening to you, so you decided that in this life you would be quiet. Maybe you were guilty of treason and told secrets that caused other people to die. Or perhaps you were a big fat liar in your past life and the lies you told hurt other people a great deal. See where all of this is going? There are many variables contained within the karmic expressions of past events, attitudes, and emotions that you're experiencing now.

You become aware of your karma through the past life influences and effects that you see and feel in your present life. Look into the situations in your life, and how you feel about them, to see what your karma is. Ask yourself what you did to deserve this. Let your thoughts and feelings flow with how the present mirrors the past. When you know what your karma is—what your soul desires to learn from having this experience—you intuitively know how to balance your karma.

Karma continues from lifetime to lifetime. Influences from past life events, whether they were good or bad, affect you in the present. They appear to give you the opportunity to continue to enjoy previous experiences or to understand your negative karma so that you can balance, bless, and heal the energies from the past in the present.

BETTER BALANCING

When you balance your karma, you're changing your present feelings about the events of the past to reshape what you're feeling and experiencing in the present. What you're doing is changing the energies of the past, and those changed energies will ripple through all the related vibrations of energy associated with the events and emotions in your past life to change what you experience now in your present life.

Balancing bad karma creates good karma. As you understand, accept, forgive, bless, and heal the past life events and emotions, and change your feelings and actions in the present, the energy surrounding the related past life event changes. This influences and affects the way the energy is manifested in your karma. The past life event doesn't change, but your attitude does, and this is what changes the energy around past life events. That energy then begins to manifest in positive ways that are reflected in your present life.

There are several ways to balance your karma, bless the experience, and heal the events of a past life. During your past life regression, you'll intuitively know how to balance your karma, bless, and let go of situations, emotions, and other souls—to release and heal them in loving ways. Your higher self will be there to help you and guide you through the balancing process. When the experience and/or emotions are healed, you will feel a wonderful and beautiful release. The soul healing will be experienced first in your feelings and then reflected in the events in your present life.

One way to balance your karma is through forgiveness. Forgiveness truly balances and heals karma. Forgiveness is sometimes difficult to do because you may need to face, very honestly and directly, some awful things you've done in the past or some awful things other people have done to you. To balance your karma in this manner, you need to either forgive yourself or the other person, according to what the situation warrants. In many situations, you need to forgive both yourself and the other person, and any other souls who were involved. Forgiveness, to be effective, needs to be done sincerely through your feelings and from your soul.

At all times while balancing your karma, be true to your feelings. If you're not ready to balance, or feel you can't balance, there's always a good reason for it. You may need to experience the karma in a more in-depth way to learn from it, or you may only need to look within the karmic situation to understand it better, and to see how you're growing your soul. Work with your feelings in the way that is most appropriate for you.

As you balance your karma, you may need to do it in small steps rather than in one leap. It depends on what the karma is and how attached you are to it. Sometimes you can't balance it all in one fell swoop. You may still need to experience the effects of it to learn some soul lessons. Karma is a good thing; it shows you what your soul desires to experience and learn; it helps you evolve your soul.

Once your karma is balanced, or is in the process of being balanced, it's important to do a healing on both the present and the related past life emotions and events. There are several ways to heal the energies of karma. One way is to use the pure, positive, powerful energies of white light to surround the events and emotions of a particular past life and their interrelated effects in your present life. This energy will then allow positive, loving energies into the present, where you can follow through with positive actions.

You intuitively know, on a soul level, what needs to be done. You'll become aware of the most appropriate way for you to heal your karma by allowing your higher self to show you how, and to help you heal a particular event or an entire lifetime. You'll instinctively gravitate toward healing because this is the nature of your soul, and your soul desires balance and harmony.

During your past life journey, you'll be seeing important events you participated in that caused and created your present karma; you'll receive an understanding of their relevance to and influence on your present life. The scripted portion directs you to balance and heal your karma in the most appropriate way during the regression, based on what the situation is, your feelings about it, and the advice of your higher self, who has a higher access to the whole picture and will share that information with you.

It's important to release and completely let go of the negative energies of karma, and then do a healing on both the past life event and the related present situation where the karma is expressing itself. It's just as important to heal the present as it is to heal the past. The reason for healing past and present events and your emotions is to cleanse and purge any remaining negativity so that no remnants are left behind. By healing the present event, the energies that surround past life events change to reflect the positive resolution of karma, and vice versa. Then it's no longer karma; it's a learning experience that has helped your soul to grow and evolve.

THE PROCESS OF POSITIVE CHANGE

You can change the energies of past life experiences in any way you choose. You can make it better or you can make it worse. I'm guessing that you'll go the positive route. Your present feelings and the positive actions you follow through with will change the energies of the past, affect and alter the present, and modify your future.

Balancing karma is a four-step process. It begins with your desire to change. This is the first step in balancing. The second step is accepting and understanding both your past and present emotions, the events involved in what you want to balance, and knowing why you want to achieve balance. This shows you how you're evolving your soul.

The third step is changing your feelings and perceptions in a positive manner about both the present and the corresponding past life events and emotions by seeing the positive aspects of the past/present experiences—by looking at what you've learned and the benefits you've gained by having the past/present experiences—and deciding what you want to do about them. The fourth step is the efforts and actions you take to balance your karma in your present life. Making new, positive changes in your thoughts, feelings, and actions completes the process of balancing; the negative event becomes a positive event because you perceive it in a positive manner.

It's very important to balance your karma by moving toward what you want, rather than moving away from what you don't want. If you're moving away from what you don't want, you're directing your energy in a negative way. Your results will follow the flow of your energy. If you balance your karma in a negative way or for the wrong reasons, you'll find that the negative is what you end up with.

For example, let's say the karma you want to balance involves a rotten relationship. You dump the relationship by walking away from it. For a time it appears that you're done with it, even though this leaves you with bad feelings about it. Because of your feelings, and by not resolving the negativity, your next relationship develops in much the same way and becomes similar to your original relationship. By moving *away* from what you don't want, you get what you wanted to get rid of.

When you move *toward* what you want, you direct your energy in a positive manner and experience positive results. You begin to balance your karma by understanding your feelings about what you want to change in the relationship and why you want to change it. You then change your thoughts and feelings to reflect what you want, and you decide whether to keep the relationship or let it go. If you keep it, you put positive changes into action. If you let it go, you do it in a positive manner. Either way, this gives you good feelings about it and you've allowed yourself to grow and learn from the experience. When you balance in this way, you're moving toward what you want.

SIDETRACKS . . .
Present Purposes

What holds true for balancing and healing your karma from the past also holds true for your actions in the present. In addition to balancing your karma and healing events from your past lives, it's important to balance present events and emotions before they turn into karma that will follow you around. As you balance and heal emotions, situations, and relationships in your present life, you change the energy and create positive experiences in your current life. It's the same process—understanding, blessing, and healing. You can supersede the occurrence of future karma by creating good vibrations in your present life.

11

PURSUING
YOUR PURPOSE

Why are you here and what are you meant to do in your life? What's your purpose this time around? Your purpose may be a combination of lessons, things that your soul desires to experience, and what you set out for yourself to achieve in the area of spiritual growth. You can have more than one purpose, but there is usually one thing you hold most dear as your heart's desire. While your karma may be an indication of what your purpose is, your purpose is usually a bit elevated or grows out of your karma.

Your purpose is almost always an ongoing process; it usually isn't the culmination of something you've achieved. It's not reaching the destination, but the journey itself that leads you to your purpose. Once you achieve your purpose, you continue on your soul's journey to expand your purpose and evolve your soul. Working toward your purpose is emotionally and spiritually fulfilling; achieving and continuing to fulfill your purpose is emotionally and spiritually rewarding.

Sometimes your purpose is a combination of physical goals and spiritual desires. Perhaps reaching a goal is a stepping-stone that will show you what your soul desires for you to accomplish. One of my friends was in the process of adopting a child from China. As she was immersed in her journey toward adoption, she became aware that there was a higher purpose within it. During her two-week stay in China to receive her child, she visited the orphanage and knew that her purpose was to help these children become adopted. She became an advocate and spokesperson for international adoptions.

One of my clients, Ann, came for a past life regression wanting to know what her purpose is in this lifetime. She felt lost, wandering, and didn't know what she was here to achieve. She felt she should be doing something but didn't know what it was. In a tearful journey, she became aware that her purpose this time is to experience being loved. In several past lives, she had been abused and rejected by her friends and family, people whom she trusted who let her down. She is with them again, loving them, and they are loving her back.

An accomplished businessman had worked long and hard to achieve the status he had acquired, but was desperately unhappy with the cutthroat tactics in the business world and felt that something important was missing in his life. At his wife's urging, he came for a past life regression, wanting to be more in touch with his soul. In a past life, he'd been very poor and hated it. The only good thing in that life, according to him, was his family.

When I guided him into the interim between lives, he became aware of a vow he'd made to himself that he never wanted to experience being poor and having to struggle again; he wanted to have lots of money and power so that he and his family could be comfortable. In this life, he had achieved that but realized that his spiritual purpose was to truly appreciate what he'd already had, and has now again, with his family. He quit his job and went into business for himself, working from home.

My main soul purpose this time is to share spiritual knowledge. That theme was in two of my past lives, where I was a spiritual teacher. In one, I refused to share what I knew, keeping it to myself. That hurt others I could have helped. By the way, one of those people I didn't help showed up in my reincarnation class and she was still angry with me. In another life—the one I experienced in Egypt as a high priest–turned–philosopher—I was supposed to keep the esoteric knowledge secret but freely spoke and wrote about it.

I balanced my karma from that first lifetime of silence in the second life of speaking what I knew to help people empower themselves. But because I had previously hurt other people by not speaking, I had to pay the karma for it, and I suffered by being tortured and then put to death, but not before I was forced to watch the words—the knowledge—that I had written on a papyrus scroll burn. This was the karmic payback for not sharing my knowledge; I wasn't allowed to share it even though I really wanted to. I chose this lifetime to share the same knowledge again; it's why I'm a writer and a teacher this time around.

One of my clients has ten children. She was sterile in a past life where she wanted more than anything to have children. Her purpose in this life is to be a mom, to experience mothering other souls. Love and children, relationships and friendships, and career are common themes in achieving the purposes your soul desires.

Sometimes your purpose shows up in a symbolic manner. Another client feels that she's on a path toward her purpose of becoming an optometrist by going to school. She wants to help people see clearly because she felt she was focused on the wrong things in a past life, in which she had closed her eyes to certain experiences and didn't clearly see what was really happening.

Many people feel they need to be on a path to pursue their purpose. There is a lot of talk about following one's path. Your path toward your spiritual purpose is simply what you do in your life that leads you to what you desire. No matter what path you take, they all lead you toward your purpose. You can discover the path you chose to follow to reach your purpose in two different ways.

If you struggle for everything you want, you're probably not following the path toward your purpose, although maybe your purpose is to struggle to achieve it. If you're following a path that is contrary to what your soul desires to accomplish, you'll find stumbling blocks along the way until you get back on the right path.

The easiest way to follow the path that your soul chose for this lifetime is to do what makes you happy and brings you joy. Honor your inner feelings of what you want to do in your life. You innately know within your heart and mind what you set out to accomplish this time. Following your purpose is finding the right path to follow. To know if your path is right for you, listen to your feelings and trust your inner knowing. When you're on the path that's right for you, you feel it on a deep, spiritual level within yourself. You know that what you want to achieve and what you're doing are the right things for you.

To know what your purpose is in this lifetime, look at what you want to do and what makes you happy. Think about what you'd like to do more than anything else; also look at what you feel you should do. If it's a bit out of your reach, notice the things that flow naturally into your life. Notice the events and experiences that make you feel as if you're on the right path, the ones that lead you toward what you want to accomplish, and the ones that show you the way. You already know, maybe subconsciously, maybe on the surface, what your purpose is.

Knowing what your purpose is, understanding why you chose your purpose, and discovering the direction of your path that will lead you to reaching your purpose, will answer the question of why you're here and what you're meant to be doing with your life this time. You're the only one who can answer this question. Look within yourself, within your heart and mind, within your past life memories, and you'll find the answer.

During your past life regression, you'll become aware of what your purpose is in this life, and what it was in previous lives. You can further explore your purpose in the following side trip that will help you open up the awareness of your purpose and show you what you're meant to be doing with your life this time around.

SIDE TRIP . . . FOLLOWING THE PATH TO YOUR PURPOSE

We all wonder what we're here to do, to accomplish, what our purpose in life is. We wonder what path to follow or if the path we're following is the right one. We wonder what path will lead us in the right direction. Yet somewhere within us, we already know what our purpose is and the path we need to follow to find it.

You're outside, walking along at a mellow pace, just enjoying your walk with no particular place to go. As you walk, you're reflecting on your thoughts, wanting to be in touch with your soul's wisdom, wanting to know what your purpose is and how to go about achieving it. You look forward in the distance, as if the answer awaits you there.

Ahead of you, you see a path with stepping-stones. You wonder if this path will lead you to your purpose, the one you chose in this lifetime that will help you evolve your soul. The end of the path isn't visible to you from where you are right now, yet somehow you know that this path will lead you into a spiritual place where you can discover what your purpose is.

Stepping onto the path, you see that you are on the rainbow mountain again, the magical, majestic mountain you explored earlier as you traveled through the rainbow to find the gifts of your soul within the energies of the colors. As you leisurely follow the path through the colors, you pause on the steps of the path within each color to remember and enjoy what your soul gave you and shared with you in each of the colors. You feel happy and peaceful within your soul. At the same time, you experience a feeling of growing joy and anticipation, knowing that there is another very special gift from your soul on this mountain for you.

As you continue along the path, you find that it leads you into the chapel that you became aware of in the color violet on the top of the mountain. You know, with a sacred knowing inside your soul, that the answer to what your purpose is in this life will be found within the chapel, within your soul. You enter your chapel, which is filled with the harmony of the vibrations of your soul to meditate on your life, to look within and to know what your purpose is this time, to remember what your soul set out for you to achieve that will bring you happiness and inner peace, that will help you to evolve your soul.

You see a delicately decorated music box that has been placed on the altar for you. Lifting the lid, you hear a beautiful melody begin to play; you know that the tones and chords you hear are the melody of your soul, flowing and resonating deep within you and all around you. The soulful, harmonious music draws you in so completely that you feel as if you are the music, as if you are the melody. The sounds are harmonious and gentle, soft and soothing, bringing you into a spiritual place of knowing within yourself. You close your eyes to more fully appreciate the music, the symphony of your soul in harmony with your soul's desires. As you listen within, you feel your awareness expanding, ever so softly and gently into the vibrations of your soul.

The music brings you to a spiritual place deep within you, into a place of spiritual knowing inside your soul. As you listen to the sounds of your soul, as you meditate on the harmony of the music and feel the vibrations of your soul, the answer to what your purpose is comes quietly to you, maybe as a whisper, or as a feeling, or as a picture you see in your mind and feel in your heart. You know, with an absolute knowing, what your soul chose to do in this life, what your soul truly desires to accomplish. You see where you are on your path toward accomplishing what you set out to do, and you see the steps before you that will lead you to fulfilling your chosen destiny.

It's been said that all of life is a journey, and that the destination itself is not the goal, rather it is the journey toward the destination and the steps along the way. Follow the joyful sounds of your soul, listen to the rhythm of your heart in tune with your inner knowing, and travel lightly toward fulfilling your purpose with a song in your heart.

PART IV

JOURNEYING

12

MIND-TRIPPING

There are many ways to experience a past life regression. Sometimes it's easier to do a past life regression if it's something you've done before, as you'll be more comfortable and familiar with the experience. Mind-tripping is something you've done many times before, most recently in some of the meditations in this book.

You've also mind-tripped every time you daydream, going somewhere else other than the present. You projected your awareness into a scene that you were not physically in. As you became totally involved with your thoughts and feelings, you may have experienced the scenes and events in your mind-trip to the extent where you felt as if you were actually involved in the scene, rather than watching it or thinking about it.

When you engage in a focused meditation or a daydream, your awareness is traveling outside yourself toward something you want to accomplish or wish would happen, or you go somewhere else in your mind to get away from where you are. Perhaps you've daydreamed about goals you want to accomplish. You see yourself in a mind picture of having attained your goal. A reverie is similar to a daydream, except you're going within your mind to see something you already know or feel to be true.

The power of your mind is truly awesome. Your thoughts and feelings can take you anywhere you want to go. Before we go any further, let me tell you that some of my clients worried about whether they would be making up the information in their past life regression. That just doesn't happen. They also wondered if what they saw during the regression was real or if they were just playing with thoughts inside their imagination.

The value of imagination has been highly underrated and grossly undermined. Your imagination is the world of your inner images; it's a wonderful resource and a powerful way into your subconscious mind. It's a doorway that frees up your subconscious mind and allows it to share its secrets with you. Your subconscious is always honest and truthful; that's simply the nature of your subconscious. It shows you your real, true feelings. When you are engaged in a past life regression, you are tapping into the soul knowledge—the truth—within your subconscious mind. You are not making it up; it's real. Your soul is showing you the experiences and emotions you've had in previous lifetimes.

Past life memories that directly affect what you're currently experiencing are very close to the surface. Your past life memories, and their corresponding images and feelings, are given to you by your subconscious mind. You already know the truth and you have the answers within. Your imagination will show you what's inside your subconscious mind.

SIDE TRIPS ... ROUNDABOUT REVERIES

Using your imagination to do a reverie about who you were, what you did, and what happened to you in a past life is a great way to open up and explore past life memories. Playing with your imagination puts you in touch with your true inner feelings. Reveries help you stretch your imagination and expand your awareness. If you think you're making it up to begin with, you'll be pleasantly surprised to see the truth in your subconscious.

The following two side trips are mini do-it-yourself past life regressions, revised from my first book on reincarnation, *Discovering Your Past Lives*. During the reveries, let the information inside your subconscious mind open up and flow naturally. Don't let your conscious mind interfere with or filter the information you become aware of. Pay special attention to your feelings about what you see in the reveries. Your feelings will help you go within your imagination, and will also help you to understand the images, thoughts, and emotions you become aware of.

Do a roundabout reverie, coming full circle from the present into the past, then returning to the present. You can remember pieces of your past lives by engaging in a reverie about who you might have been before and who you really were in one of your past lives. Your subconscious will show you the truth.

Think about the kind of person you might have been, or could have been, in a past life, based on your present feelings and current experiences. Focus on what is happening in the present to lead you into the past. Open your imagination and explore the possibilities. What you think of as a possibility may turn into a probability because your subconscious knows the truth and this is one of the many ways that your knowing mind shares information with you.

Let your thoughts run free; set your imagination free. Pretend you're someone else. See how he/she is dressed and what he/she is doing. Notice the environment around him/her and what is happening. Think his/her thoughts and feel his/her emotions. Let yourself be really free as you flow with this reverie. You'll find that who you think you were is probably who you really were. See yourself as who you were before. See everything that is happening; be in all the scenes from your past life as you feel your emotions and listen to your thoughts.

Bring this past life awareness into your present life, seeing and understanding all the connections, and how your past experiences and feelings have influenced the present, shaping the person you are now and the experiences you have. See how the past intertwines with the present, creating what you're experiencing now in your life.

Do another reverie, but this time with a focused direction. You may have found yourself in situations where you've thought, "What did I do in a past life to deserve this!?" Take this one step further. What do you think you did to deserve what you got? Open your imagination to find the answers by looking within your mind. Karma is always just and fair; you always get what you deserve. You've already asked yourself this question in the karma chapter, but maybe you haven't answered it yet. You did a similar mind-trip in Chapter Three, in the intuitive insights journey, as you were looking for similarities between the past and the present. This side trip may expand on what you became aware of in that mind-trip.

Take a deep breath and relax. Let your conscious mind become quiet. As you relax and become centered within yourself, you'll enter a meditative frame of mind. Think about something in your life that is troubling you that you'd like to get to the bottom of so you can understand why it is happening.

Ask yourself what you did in a past life to deserve this. Let go of any preconceived ideas, thoughts, feelings, judgments, and rationalizations. Open up your imagination. Let it flow with the images, thoughts, and feelings of what you might have done or experienced in a past life that caused and created what you're experiencing now. Go with the flow of what appears in your mind.

Your karma will take you directly into a past life. This is because the energies of past and present events are closely connected. While karma was created in a past life, the energies of it flow into what you're experiencing now in the present. Instead of traveling on your thoughts and feelings, you traveled on the energy of karma.

SIDE TRIPS . . . TRIPPING THROUGH TIME

You can practice a past life regression, staying close to the present by exploring and experiencing a present life memory. This helps you get the feel of a mind-trip as a prelude to your past life journey. As your awareness travels outside the immediate present and you go into the memory, notice the feelings and sensations you experience, the thoughts and images you become aware of, and how you become aware of them. Notice your thoughts and feelings before, during, and after your mind-trip, and the way that you physically respond to the memory as you project your awareness into the previous event.

For your practice trip, enter a meditative frame of mind. Go into your spiritual sanctuary and connect with your higher self. From there, project your thoughts to a place you've been before in this life. Remember a pleasant and happy time you experienced there. Watch yourself experiencing the event, then completely project your awareness into seeing, feeling, and reexperiencing the previous event. Be aware of all your earlier thoughts and feelings when you experienced the event for the first time. Become totally involved in the scene as you see, sense, and feel the images of your memory. Let your higher self guide you and explain everything you're experiencing.

View your memory two ways, from two different perspectives. First, view the scene objectively, in a detached manner. Just imagine that you're watching a movie and observe the action. Then, be in the scene. Be the person you were when this event occurred. Experience it subjectively, with your feelings, as you participate in it. Really feel the emotions that you felt before. Completely experience all the sights, sounds, and scenes around you.

Be aware of what you experience and feel in both perspectives—the first from the outside in, and the second from the inside out. The same experience, viewed in two different ways, gives you an overall, in-depth understanding of the previous experience. This is the same way that you'll be viewing and experiencing the events and emotions in your past lives during the regression.

When you're done with your practice trip, slowly focus on the present. Gradually bring your awareness into your present surroundings in the present time, remembering all your feelings and experiences on your present life mind-trip. Reflect on everything you saw and felt, and all the information you became aware of. Take a few moments to completely absorb all the information you received, then fully orient yourself into the present. By moving slowly from the past through the transition of time into the present, you'll retain more information on a conscious level and understand it better.

Take another mind-trip into the past but go a bit further this time. Travel into a place where you feel you've lived before in a past life. Journey into the past with a specific place in mind. Knowing your destination helps you arrive there. Your soul knows where it wants to go. It will be interesting for you to see if you've lived there and what you learned that you can now bring into your present life.

Mind-trip into a past life, to see and remember what your soul knows. For a starting point, choose a place that you feel an affinity for, a place where you feel you might have lived in a past life, or a place you feel drawn to that you'd like to visit to see if you've had a previous incarnation there. You might want to expand on the information you became aware of in the first roundabout reverie.

When you have a place in mind, choose an image or a symbol that, for you, represents the place you want to visit. Choose a symbol that you feel is appropriate for you or let your higher self show you an image. For example, if you feel that you were an American Indian in a past life, you might see an image of moccasins or a teepee. If you were a gladiator in ancient Rome, you might see a chariot or the armor that you wore. If you lived in Egypt, you might see a pyramid or a sphinx.

Create or allow an image to appear in your subconscious mind and focus on it to see where it leads you. Remember that your subconscious speaks to you in symbols, so this is a perfect way to draw you into a past life. Choosing a symbol for your subconscious mind to follow or allowing your subconscious to show you a past life image will align your awareness with the past life that the symbol represents.

If you're the least bit apprehensive about journeying into the past or a little worried that nothing will come to you and you won't go anywhere, consider these two things: Having a general idea of where you're going will help you get there, and focusing on an image to start your journey will open related scenes in your past lives.

Begin your trip into a past life by entering a meditative frame of mind. Relax and go through the rainbow. Breathe in and surround yourself with the white light protection. Go into your spiritual sanctuary and focus on the image that represents a place where you've lived before. Your higher self is there with you and will guide you as you focus on and project your awareness into the image. Center your awareness on the image that represents the place you choose to visit. This will be the beginning of your mind-trip as you project your thoughts and feelings into a specific place and point in time in one of your past lives.

The image you choose as a focal point, or the image that your higher self shows you, or the one that appears in your mind, will direct you to where you've lived before and show you an important event you experienced there that affects you now. Picturing the image in your mind, you feel yourself being drawn to an important event you experienced before. When you arrive, take a few moments to become aware of the scene, to see what the landscape is like, to familiarize yourself with what is happening, and to understand why it is happening. Watch your past life play out as you watch yourself participate in it.

As you enter the place in time where you lived before, and you see the scene, completely project your thoughts and feelings into where you are. See and feel yourself as you were before. See how you're dressed and what you're doing. Be aware of the sights and sounds that are around you. Be aware of the situation you are in. Be very aware of your thoughts and feelings. Discover things you've known before and what you've done before. Discover who you were before. With your higher self guiding you and answering all your questions, fully explore and experience the significant events and emotions in your past life. Take all the time you want to completely immerse yourself in the experiences in the past life you've become aware of.

When you're done with this side trip, return to your spiritual sanctuary with your higher self to absorb and assimilate the information you became aware of. Reflect on everything you experienced during your mind-trip, on your thoughts and feelings as you observed and/or participated in your past life, and all the insights and understanding you received as you saw who you were before and what you experienced. Notice the connections and similarities between the events in your past life that are reflected in the present, how the memory relates to your present life, and how and why the memory you experienced can help you in your present life. You can ask your higher self for the answers.

After your reflections, slowly bring your awareness into the present time by focusing and directing your thoughts and feelings into who you are now and where you are right now. As you orient yourself in the present, bring with you the awareness of everything you've seen and experienced, and all the knowledge you've acquired about your past life that provides you with insight and understanding into your present life.

These roundabout reveries and your practice trips show you that you can easily enter your past life memories to become aware of who you were before and what you've done, to see what happened to you and to understand why it happened, and how all of this relates to your present life.

13

TRAVELING
THROUGH TIME

Time becomes irrelevant when you journey into the past. The events and emotions in your past lives aren't affected by time. The energies that surround past life events and emotions survive in the present. This is due to the flow of energy that filters through time, because of the influence the past life has on your present life. When you remember and reexperience the things that occurred in your past lives, you blend the energies of past and present events and emotions together. Because you're placing your awareness into your past life, and seeing its effect on your present life, the energies of time are interconnected between the past and the present.

On your past life journey, you'll be mind-tripping through time into your memories. When you mind-trip, you're placing your thoughts and feelings—your awareness—somewhere other than the present, into another place, another time, and you're remembering and reexperiencing events and emotions you've experienced before. You're traveling on the energy of your thoughts and feelings. As you journey into and through your past lives, you'll see and feel past life events and emotions that relate to and have an influence on your present life by viewing and experiencing them from different perspectives and through different perceptions.

You can experience what occurred in your past lives either as a participant or as an observer, or you can do both at the same time. The manner in which you perceive the experiences and emotions in your past lives will depend on what is happening in the memory. You can journey into your past lives without feeling the emotions, you can relive the events and emotions, or you can get an overview by watching yourself participate in the scene from above the scene.

If you choose to be an observer, you'll be emotionally removed from the feelings and experiences while you remain involved in the scene. You'll be watching the scenes in your mind and they'll have a dreamlike quality. You'll be aware of your feelings and the events in a detached manner, as if they are happening to someone else. If you choose to be a participant, you'll be directly involved in feeling the emotions and experiencing the events in your past life memories. Your awareness will be completely absorbed in the scene, in everything you're feeling and everything that is happening. You'll be totally there in heart, mind, and soul.

If you choose to be a participant and an observer at the same time, your awareness will be above the past life event as you watch yourself participate in it. You'll be aware of everything and your understanding of what you experience in the event will be expanded; you'll see beyond what you're feeling and experiencing, and get an overall picture of what is happening and why it is happening. You'll understand the reasons why the event occurred and why you acted the way you did through the eyes and awareness of your higher self. This gives you an increased understanding of the origins of the event—how and why it happened—and the reasons for and purpose of your previous actions and reactions.

Past and Present Purposes

You can use these three perspectives in your daily life to help you in many positive ways. The manner in which you'll be seeing and experiencing your past life memories can also be used to help you gain an overall picture and expanded perspective in viewing experiences and situations in your present life to help you make clearer choices and decisions, and to gain a better understanding of these situations and experiences.

Open your perceptions and explore your intuition and inner knowing within these perspectives. You can read situations that are currently happening by employing an overview of all that is happening, much in the same way that you'll be using these perspectives to gain perceptive insight and intuitive information inside your past life memories. You can mind-trip into your present experiences to gain insight and find ways to resolve problems, whether they originated in a past life or in your present life. This can also help you avoid incurring present karma that will appear in the future. You can get to the cause of the present-day problem and resolve it in a positive manner. By healing the present, you simultaneously heal the past.

If you have a problem, enter a meditative frame of mind and be in touch with your higher self. Look at the higher, overall picture of why the problem is occurring. Go inside the problem, be above the problem, be outside the problem, be the problem, and see what you discover. You can then resolve the problem and use white light to help you heal the problem and your emotions that are connected with it. This is what you'll be doing in your past life regression as you become aware of what your karma is and the best way to balance and heal it.

THINGS TO KNOW BEFORE YOU GO

The past lives you remember and reexperience will be the ones that relate to and are important to your present life. As you explore and reexperience the past, you'll see the connections between the past and the present, and how they're interwoven. Your past life regression is an informative and enlightening journey of self-discovery. You'll see who you were before and how events and emotions in your past lives influence, interact with, and affect your present situations, relationships, and feelings.

There are certain things to become aware of and important items to look for that will place you more directly in the scene and help you become more involved in your past life memory. When you first enter your past life memory, familiarize yourself with where you are and what you're doing. Observe what is happening. This will help you orient yourself and find your focus as you start your travels. Notice whether you're male or female, a child or an adult. You can make an educated guess as to your age. See the clothes you're wearing and look at your hands to see the color of your skin. Touch your clothes to feel their texture. Look at your feet to see what type of shoe or foot covering you have on. As you look at your feet, you become aware, symbolically, of the path you've traveled in your previous life.

Take in all the sights and scenery around you to see where you are. Be aware of any noises or smells. Look at the landscape to see what it is like. Notice what the weather is like. This sensory information will place you more directly in the scene, open up more details, and may give you geographical information; it will also help acclimate you as you go inside your memory.

See if someone is with you or if you're alone. If someone is with you, he/she may call you by name. Notice what you're doing, how you're feeling, and what your thoughts are. Pay attention to any other visual and sensory information you receive. However, don't be overly concerned with details, such as names and dates or geographical data. If you focus on gaining this information right away, you'll pull yourself out of your past life memory because you'll be consciously searching for it, rather than letting yourself become subconsciously aware of it. This information will come to you in the course of your regression, as the events unfold.

The beginning steps into your past life memory may be slow and hesitant. To begin with, you may zip in and out of images and feelings before you center in clearly on one event. This may also occur at any time during your past life journey. Focus on the first things you see and become aware of. They will lead you further into the past life you're exploring. These images and feelings are important and are all interrelated. They may appear and give you glimpses or a sense of events in your past life before the full-blown memory shows itself in its entirety.

If your images and feelings are a bit fuzzy at first, don't worry about it. Just be there. Accept what you see and feel in the way that you become aware of it. The more involved you become with seeing and feeling what's going on around you—what is happening to you, how you're feeling about it, and putting yourself into the picture—the clearer your images and feelings will be and you'll become aware of even more information.

If you don't see the images clearly, simply sense them. Allow yourself to become aware of past life events through feeling them rather than seeing them. You will gain the same amount of information from feeling past life experiences as you will from seeing them. This may either be a slow start to opening up your past life memory or the feeling itself is the key to seeing the past life event. Center in and focus on your feeling. See what related feelings come into your awareness. You'll be able to determine whether the feeling is a key that opens the doorway into the past life experience or if it is a feeling that you need to tune in to more completely and clearly. Your feelings are an important part of navigating through your past life journey. Pay attention to them.

Keep in mind that time doesn't matter or have any meaning inside your memory, though you'll often see and experience events in sequence. Don't be at all surprised if the images of your memory show themselves in a time span that isn't linear. This will occur because the energies of certain events and emotions are linked; the vibrations of the images you see will appear in perfect order. They will appear in the order that is related to the event, not necessarily the order in which they occurred, or even in a linear sequence of lives. They may also appear in the order that you are ready to see them and to understand them.

As you are traveling into and through your past lives, go entirely with the flow of your memories and what you experience. Many times, things will appear to be out of sync or to make no sense. Don't judge or second-guess or struggle against what you become aware of. These memories, images, and feelings are being shown to you for a very specific reason and purpose that will unfold in perfect harmony.

As you go further into your past life memory, the images or scenes may seem to be disconnected or unrelated. This can occur for several reasons. Your subconscious mind might be jumping around a bit to find the appropriate past life memory to show you, or you may not be accepting and focusing on what you become aware of because you feel it isn't important or you don't yet understand its relevance.

This is most often caused by moving from one event into another event that relates to a central experience, and by traveling between lifetimes to become aware of interconnected events that relate to the main event. These are pivot points that revolve around a pivotal, central event or emotion. These pivot points keep you focused on the main experience or emotion; they're like an interwoven thread of energy that connects all related aspects of the past life event and/or emotion together. From this pivot point, you can turn in any direction and travel through the interrelated energies of the events to see all the aspects of the central experience that are connected to the pivotal event or emotion you're experiencing inside your memory.

If you feel a little confused by this, don't try to consciously understand what you're experiencing or to make sense of it when you first become aware of it by looking for a clear connection. This will pull you out of your memory because you'll be trying to consciously analyze it. Accept what you become aware of in the way you become aware of it, knowing that the connection will clearly reveal itself when the time is right. Sometimes these connections become clear as you progress through additional events in your past life memories, but you may receive this understanding after the session is over and you've had time to mull over the information you've become aware of during the regression.

By using your pivot points to travel through the interrelated events in one or more lifetimes, you become aware of the interweaving energies. These energies may show themselves as strands or threads of light to travel, but you'll more often experience them as a feeling or a sense of knowing. You can relate interconnected past experiences with your present experiences to understand how they interact with and influence each other by tuning in completely to your feelings.

You'll see the important scenes and situations, and feel the emotions you've had in your past lives; you'll understand their connection with and influence on one another, and how they affect the experiences in your present life. You'll receive this understanding either during your past life journey as your higher self explains it to you or after the regression when you spend time reflecting in your spiritual sanctuary. You may also become aware of connections in your dreams and through moments of meditation after the regression, or the interrelated energies may appear in a current situation when that present situation clicks and connects with a past life event.

If you're stuck or stalled in a memory and want to move on, ask your higher self why you're there and what it is that you're to learn from this particular event. Linger for a bit to see what comes to you. If no information arrives in your mind, ask to be guided to another event in that lifetime or in another lifetime that is significant and important. The thought itself will move you.

If you're wandering or need a clearer sense of direction, give yourself prompts by asking your higher self questions, such as "Where am I now? Why am I here? What am I doing here? Why am I doing it? What is my purpose here? What is the importance of this situation? What is the reason for this experience? Why am I aware of this event, emotion, feeling, or experience?" Ask other pertinent questions. Be gentle in your search for answers, not demanding. These questions, and the answers, will keep you focused on and connected to what's occurring. They'll help you to clearly orient yourself into the memory you're in, and to gain the most information and understanding from this event in your past life.

At all times during your past life journey, go with whatever you're experiencing and feeling; follow the flow of the memory and the guidance of your higher self. Listen to your thoughts and feelings; this is your higher self speaking to you and providing you with all the information you want and need to know. Completely see and sense all the images in your past life memory. Tune in to your feelings. Explore and experience everything you become aware of. Everything you see and feel inside your past life memory is significant.

During your past life journey, there is no need to rush. Time doesn't matter inside your memories, so take your time to fully experience every thought, image, and feeling you encounter. Completely explore all the events and situations you become aware of. Give yourself plenty of time to converse with your higher self, to ask questions about why you're experiencing a certain event and what its relevance is to your present life. Take all the time you need to understand what you are experiencing.

In your past lives, you'll find some happy and pleasant memories and you'll also find some that aren't so nice. You may have done a few bad things or experienced events that were painful and traumatic; the emotions from these events may still affect you. Don't skip over them; get involved with them, but respect your feelings as to how far you want to go into the memory. Sometimes it's very beneficial to reexperience the memory and completely feel your emotions from the past to help you understand what occurred and why it occurred, to clearly see how it affected you in the past and how it is affecting you in the present, and to help you heal it from the inside out.

If you come across anything painful or traumatic that you'd rather not be emotionally involved in, simply surround yourself with white light. Call for it and white light will immediately be there to surround you and the situation you're experiencing. Remember that you also have several perspectives and views available to you. You can be in the scene, above the scene, or removed from it while still being completely aware of everything that is occurring.

If your mind goes blank or the scene goes black, you may be tripping into something you're not quite ready to see or deal with. This most often occurs with severe past life pain or trauma. Your fear will cut you off from the memory. Don't let the fear get the better of you. Ask your higher self what you need to do to become aware of the event, or to explain your fear to you and the reasons why you're not able to fully see and feel this event or emotion. Don't push it. If you're not aware of what is prompting the fear or the blackout, there's a really good reason for it that you will understand at another time, perhaps after the regression while you are reflecting on it or in a dream.

If you try to forge past the fear of remembering and seeing the past life pain or trauma you experienced before you're ready to accept and understand it, you'll pop yourself out of your past life memory. Just surround yourself with white light and move on. You may next become aware of a past life event that will help to explain the fear or you may simply move on to another important event that is unrelated to the pain or trauma that your soul has experienced.

If you are feeling any present physical pain or discomfort, immediately remove yourself emotionally from the past life scene and surround yourself with white light. You can stay within the memory without feeling any pain or discomfort. If you still feel uncomfortable, just breathe and be for a few moments, or go into your spiritual sanctuary to regroup and/or do a healing with white light on the past-present event and the associated emotions, and then return to the scene to simply observe what is happening to the person you were in a detached manner as you allow yourself to understand it.

Going through the death scene seems to be highly traumatic for many people, either because of a violent death in the past or because of the fear of letting go of a physical body. Death is feared and that fear may carry over into the death scene in your past life. Your emotions are very powerful. If you feel any fear or trepidation as you approach your death in a past life, surround yourself with white light. Your soul is immortal and continues through time. Only the physical body dies; your soul survives.

Some people, when experiencing their death scene in a past life, just can't believe that they're really dead; they want to linger close to the physical body they lived in before because they still feel very attached to it and identify with it. If you feel any reluctance as your spirit leaves the past physical body, take your time with this and experience it to the extent you want to. A few people want to hang around to see what their friends and loved ones in the past did when they died and to hover over their funeral. Some people want to stay close to their loved ones in the past and are reluctant to leave them. This often occurs when young children are left behind.

Most people easily leave the body behind that housed their soul in a past life. Some are aware of going into a beautiful, radiant white light and traveling through a tunnel or walking over a bridge as they cross over to the other side. Others simply sense their soul leaving the physical body like a deep sigh, an outbreath or an exhale. Rebirthing into their spiritual essence is a wonderful, beautiful feeling of coming home that is filled with joy and happiness, and is usually accompanied by a great sense of relief to let go of the physical, especially if the past life body was old or infirm.

Once the physical body is let go of, your soul will enter the interim between lives, which is like a state of mind or a place of pure spiritual awareness, where you will experience a past life review of the lives you've become aware of in your regression. You'll receive a clear understanding of all the events that occurred; you'll know how and why they happened, how and why you responded the way you did then, and you'll become aware of the purpose that your soul set out for you to achieve in that lifetime. This is similar to what your higher self will be explaining to you during the regression. Some people, after letting go of the past physical body, enter a beautiful garden of peace and harmony to rest their soul before they experience the past life review. (More information is given on the interim between lives in Chapter Sixteen.)

The most important thing during your past life journey is to completely explore and experience all that you see and feel, and everything that your higher self shows you. As you're remembering and reexperiencing your past life, your higher self will direct and guide you to all the events that will show you everything that is important and relevant for you to know. Your higher self will explain everything you're experiencing and give you the full understanding of how the events and emotions in your past lives relate to your present life, and the reasons for becoming aware of them now. Your higher self will show you how to balance your karma from past life events, and how to heal and bless those experiences.

Take your time and go slowly through your past life journey. Pause whenever you want to, whenever it feels right to stop for a few moments to completely explore what you've become aware of, to have your higher self fully explain it to you, or stop for a while to simply take the time to breathe and regroup.

14

TRAVEL TIPS

When you're remembering scenes from your past lives and seeing the events contained within them, you'll experience rapid eye movement (REM). Rapid eye movement occurs because you're using your mind's eye to see the scenes. This is very similar to what occurs when you dream or engage in a meditative visualization, as you watch the images move in your mind. REM is a natural part of your past life regression.

In addition to experiencing REM to see past life events, eye movements can help you maneuver in your past life regression. There are a few little tricks you can employ to go into either the past or the future (to move backward or forward in time), to deepen your level of awareness, to bring yourself out immediately should you need a quick exit to rapidly return to the present, and to reenter your past life memory if you are disturbed during your past life regression.

If you want to move backward in time to something in the past, move your eyes to the left. This is also helpful if you want to return to a previous event you've already explored to experience it in greater depth in order to gain more information. If you want to move forward in a memory or travel into another memory in a progressive order, move your eyes to the right. If you want to go more deeply into your memory, roll your eyes upward, as if you are looking into your forehead. This will deepen your level of relaxation and increase your level of subconscious awareness. Rolling your eyes upward also allows you to remain inside the past life memory if you're disturbed or become distracted, and to return there easily.

Depending on the environment you are in when you journey into your past lives, you may hear outside noises, such as traffic or your neighbors, or a dog barking. Don't let these become a distraction and pull you out of your memory. Tell yourself before you begin that any outside noises you hear or become aware of will help you go deeper within your memory. At times, an outside noise may blend in with what you are experiencing or help you focus on something related inside your memory. If you are bothered by the distraction, simply breathe through it and remain calm. Stay inside your memory until the noise passes.

There may be times during your past life regression when you will need to come back immediately, with full conscious awareness, into the present. If you're interrupted during your past life regression by the phone ringing, someone knocking on your door, or for some other reason, flutter your eyelids very rapidly for a few seconds before you open your eyes.

This allows you to completely reorient yourself to the present with full alertness, and without a sudden jarring or jolt because of the rapid change in brain-wave frequencies, which is a revibration of energies; it allows a smooth transition from your subconscious mind to your conscious mind. You'll also be able to remember more of what you experienced, instead of losing most of it, as would occur in a rapid transition through the energies. You want to return clearheaded and alert, not foggy and fuzzy. If you just open your eyes, your awareness will be rapidly traveling from the past into the present; this can cause a brief and temporary disorientation, like waking up from sleep too fast.

There are several other ways to instantly bounce back into the present if you need to return quickly to full conscious awareness from your past life regression and want a smooth transition. One way is to wrap yourself completely in white light as you travel quickly into the present. Simply call out for white light and it will be there. Another way is to let your higher self instantaneously blend the past with the present. At any time during your past life regression, tell your higher self to enfold your energies and return you to the present, while keeping your full awareness of the past.

To return to where you were in your past life journey when you were interrupted, leave a marker in your past life. When you continue with your past life regression, you will return to that exact scene or situation, as if you had not been interrupted, and pick up where you left off. To create a marker, focus on an image in the scene or a feeling in the event you're experiencing. Plant that image and/or feeling in your mind. When you're ready to continue, simply take a few deep breaths, roll your eyes upward, surround yourself with white light, and envision or remember that image or feeling.

Some bodily sensations you may become aware of and experience as you travel into the past are increased saliva and the need to swallow more often; this is natural and is due to being deeply relaxed. Your breathing will slow down and deepen, much as it does when you gently fall asleep at night. You might want to have a light blanket nearby to cover you in case you feel chilled since your body temperature may drop just a bit, as it does naturally when you're very relaxed. And one more delicate matter you need to know: You won't be able to completely relax physically, or to fully open up your subconscious awareness if you have to go to the bathroom. So it might be wise to do this before you begin.

As you journey into your past lives, you will more than likely experience some of the same physical responses, to a greater degree, that you felt during the relaxation/rainbow meditations. You may feel a pleasant sensation of warmth or you may feel a bit cool. Your body may feel heavy, expansive, or very light. You may experience a sensation or feeling of floating or flying.

As you travel further into the past, you may feel as if you're moving through various shapes, such as a tunnel with rainbow-colored hues and muted lights. You may see blurred images that dart back and forth, and hear pleasant sounds that rush or swish by you. You may feel as if you're moving through soft, puffy clouds or a luminous mist. You might hear beautiful tones of harmonious music or the sound of softly tinkling bells or the gentle motion of wind chimes. This occurs because you're traveling through time and accessing ever-increasing vibrations of universal energy.

Your body may feel as if it's vibrating with energy. You may hear a humming sound or feel a buzzing sensation around your body. You may feel as if your body is being gently pricked with efferves-cent bubbles of energy. You may hear the sound of wind roaring in your ears and experience the feeling of it moving all around you as you are traveling through time. You may feel as if you're in the center of a swirling vortex of energy. (You're not in Kansas any-more.) This occurs when you enter higher levels of spiritual awareness and you synchronize your energy with the vibrations of your astral body. You may astral project into your past lives. This is a fairly normal occurrence when you raise your level of awareness and your energy vibrations.

The difference between mind-tripping and astral projecting into past life memories is that when you are astral projecting, more of your soul's energy and essence is invested in and involved with the scenes you are reexperiencing. Your soul is actually there. When you're mind-tripping, your subconscious awareness is in your past life memories and you're exploring them more on a physical level rather than on a spiritual level.

The sights, sounds, feelings, and images you become aware of—the soft blurs of light, the muted sounds, and the frequencies of energy—may occur at any time during your regression as you travel through the vibrations of time and energy. All these feelings are normal and natural. You may experience none of them, some of them, or all of them, in varying degrees. You may also experience other things that are not listed here as you travel through time and spiritual energies. Keep in mind that all these sensations will be pleasant and comfortable for you, and make for a more interesting journey along the way.

When you return to your present physical energies, you may feel as if you're moving through layers of energy; as you enter the present, these layers may feel heavier or denser. This is because both time and physical energy vibrate at a slower rate than spiritual energy. You may experience, in reverse, what you felt in a more spiritual frame of mind as you traveled toward your past life memories. As you return to the present, you're exchanging spiritual energies for physical energies.

As you're returning to the present from the past, stop for a while in your spiritual sanctuary to reflect on what you experienced, and to more completely understand the events and emotions you became aware of during your past life journey. You may choose to rest there for a while, to refresh and replenish yourself, if your journey was a bit traumatic, or to gather the information you've received to fully incorporate it into your conscious awareness. You may also want your higher self to help you balance and heal any karma in your sanctuary that wasn't healed during the regression, and to bless the experiences and let them go.

As you return to the present, through the rainbow colors in reverse, take your time and move slowly from the past into the present, feeling the various vibrations of energy as you travel completely into the present. Take the time to revibrate your energies to the present here and now, and to fully reorient yourself into the present, into who you are right now. Moving slowly from the past into the present enables you to remember all that you experienced on your past life journey and to retain it on a conscious level.

KEYS AND CLUES

During your past life regression, you may become aware of symbols or images that represent something you need to understand before the memory surfaces. They may show up as clues and leads to follow in your past life journey. You may have become aware of some of these symbols or images when you explored the imprints and impressions of your soul in Chapter Three. These same imprints of your past lives may surface during your journey to act as a trigger or a key into fully opening your memory.

Very few of my clients have experienced this during a past life regression, but since it may happen, it's a good idea to know how to best deal with it. The symbols and images you may become aware of are similar to the symbols you sometimes see in your dreams and the imagery that appears in your mind when you meditate or engage in a reverie. Your subconscious offers you these mind pictures to help you understand what it is trying to tell you and show you that it cannot express in words or through feelings.

Your subconscious speaks in symbols and imagery, translating words into pictures. It does its best to help you connect the pictures you see in your mind with a word so you can understand the spiritual symbols and imagery that may appear in your past life regression and use them as clues and keys to open the understanding of what you're really seeing and what your soul is saying to you.

You may also become aware of symbols that represent something you're not yet ready to see and experience. The symbol hides what's inside your memory. Once you understand the symbol's meaning, you may be able to open up the past life memory or you may need to ponder it a bit further before the memory will open up. These symbols may either be keys or gatekeepers, opening up the doorway into discovering your past lives or keeping the memory locked away from you until you're ready to accept it, understand it, and explore it.

You can uncover the clues and keys to your past life memory by understanding what the symbols and images represent to you. This is very similar to deciphering dream symbols, with one huge exception. When you're trying to understand nighttime dreams, you're in a conscious level of mind; this impedes the interpretation because the symbols are given to you in a subconscious level of mind. When you try to decipher what they mean, you're doing it in a different level of mind than the one in which they were given to you. Subconscious images don't translate well into conscious pictures. When you're seeing imagery and symbolism during your past life regression, you're already in your subconscious mind and can easily interpret and understand the keys and clues.

An easy way to understand what the symbol or imagery represents in a past life is to ask your higher self or think about what it means to you on a feeling level. Your higher self can tell you what the spiritual symbolism is and what it means within the picture that your mind draws for you. Remember that during your past life journey, you're tuned in to your spiritual awareness and you have complete access to your inner knowing.

Here are a few examples of how to understand the symbols and images you see, and to follow the clues and leads in your past life memory. One of my clients, upon first entering her past life memory, became aware of a tall white building. There were no other structures around this gleaming white building, so I instructed her to go inside the building. She said there were no doors. I suggested that perhaps the building was symbolic and that she could fashion a door so that she could go into the building where she would find her past lives.

She struggled to create a door, but wasn't having any success. However, as she walked around the building, she noticed that there was a window on the other side, but it was closed and locked. She said that the sunlight glinting off it created a pattern of trees. I asked her what trees represented to her. She said that she was a tomboy when she was a child and used to climb trees to get away from the neighborhood bullies.

She realized that she was afraid of what she might see in her past lives and wanted the security of a tree to climb in case whatever was in her past life memory tried to overpower her. I asked her to imagine that the building was really a tall tree with many branches that she could climb on. I mentioned that when she had seen the gleaming white building and the sunlight reflecting off the window, she had already surrounded her past life memories in white light. The image in her mind changed into a tree of light, and she was able to continue on her past life journey.

Sometimes it's easy to figure out the symbolism. Your subconscious will clearly present the obvious. Another client was having trouble keeping the scene he was exploring in focus while he was trying to balance his karma. The images in the scene kept going from shades of gray to black and white, and then bursting into full color. When he saw gray, the images in the scene were wavering and connecting. When he saw black and white, the scene was completely still and nothing was happening. When he saw color, the scene was moving almost too fast to be perceptible.

I suggested that perhaps he was ambivalent about balancing the karma because every time he tried to reconcile his past feelings with his present ones, the scene changed from black and white to color, then went into wavering shades of gray. It looked as if he wanted a clean break from his karma, to see it in black and white, but karma doesn't work that way. Karma works in shades of gray. Threads of karma weave in and around and through experiences, and there's no way to completely cut the thread. Once he accepted that there was no clear-cut division between what he did in the past and how it was affecting him in the present, the scene settled into slow-moving color images that he could relate to.

Another client saw bees buzzing around her. She tried to swat them away, but they came back in ever-increasing numbers. She ran away from them, not wanting to get stung. I asked if she'd been stung by a bee in her present life. She said no; I asked what bees represented to her. Honey was her answer. All of a sudden, a light went off for her in her mind. Honey is what she called her husband when he was alive. Even though she had come for a past life regression, the session turned into a spiritual communication between her late husband and herself. The realms you explore during a past life regression are the same realms that your spirit dwells in.

After the regression, she explained that she had been thinking about contacting a medium because she wanted to get in touch with her husband, but she was afraid. She said that when she ran away from the bees, she was afraid of being in communication with her late husband because she had been brought up to believe that once you're dead, you're dead. She didn't want to have any ghosts, even her husband's ghost, haunting her. The key word here is *being*. Her subconscious showed her bees that sting so she could make the connection with *be-ing* with her husband, who is her honey.

Sometimes the clues and leads you become aware of can be a bit difficult to unearth and follow, much like excavating ancient ruins. An elderly gentlemen came for a past life regression, wanting to know what his relationship was with his son in a past life. They hadn't spoken for years and he felt it was due to a past life influence, as well as events that had occurred in the present. He wanted to make peace with his son before it was too late to do anything about it in this life.

He was halfway through the regression, having explored several events that helped him understand his current personality and how it was shaped by events and emotions in several of his past lives when I instructed him to go into a past life that he had shared with his son. Upon entering the scene, which was an open field, he tripped and fell over a large rock that was embedded in the ground. He said he wasn't seeing anything in the scene except the rock that he tripped over in the dirt and some weeds; it was a barren landscape. (It seemed that he was experiencing a barren, emotionless landscape with his son in this life. I thought perhaps the rock was a barrier, or that he was only a stone's throw away from remembering.)

I asked him to focus on the rock, to talk to it and ask it why it was there, and what it meant. He began sobbing as he told me that the rock was a headstone and he was standing in an open field looking at his son's grave, regretting that he hadn't spoken to his son before he died. I surrounded him and the scene completely in white light and suggested that he just be there in spirit with his past life son to talk with him, to say the words now that he hadn't said then.

After a while, he said that he had become aware of what he had done to his son, and his son's reaction to it, in the past that created the conflict in the present. We did a healing on the past life events. He was able to forgive himself and to heal the experience, to bring the understanding into the present. I heard from him several months later; he said he was now speaking with his son. Healing the past heals the present because the energies of the past life healing travel into and affect the present.

If you run into symbols and imagery during your past life journey that you don't understand at first, don't get hung up on them or let them block you. Remember that they are keys and clues given to you from your inner knowing, from your subconscious mind, and are offered to help you along the way. Take the time you need to understand them, and to use them as keys so your past life memory can surface completely.

15

JOURNEYING INTO
YOUR PAST LIVES

Your past life journey will take you into and through previous lifetimes with a variety of experiences and emotions that come forth. Let yourself fully experience all the energies and emotions from past events. Put your whole heart and soul into it. When your journey is almost over, your higher self will guide you into the interim between lives where you will do an after-death past life review and look at the pre-birth planning your soul did for your present lifetime. This will help you understand your purpose in previous lives and what you set out to achieve in this life. These subjects are covered in greater detail in the next chapter.

The following script is a bit generic. It has to be this way because there are so many unique differences and variables in an individual's past life journey. Follow your feelings and go with what you feel drawn to pursue. The words will give you a general sense of direction. Your higher self will guide you in the most appropriate manner, directing you to all the significant events and emotions in your past lives that directly affect the situations and your feelings in your present life. Listen to yourself and let yourself go with the flow of your thoughts; follow your own inner sense of direction. Let yourself fully experience all the things you are seeing and feeling in your past life memories; give yourself all the time you need to explore and understand them.

Your Past Life Journey Continues . . .

Within the white light, you see your higher self standing there, waiting for you in your spiritual sanctuary, waiting to guide you on your past life journey. Your higher self tells you that it is time to begin your past life journey, that you are ready to explore who you were before and what you've done in lifetimes now gone by. You're ready to travel into and through your past life experiences, and to gain the knowledge of your soul. You know that all you have to do is to let your higher self direct you to the experiences in your past life or lives that are important for you to know about and understand in your present life, the past lives that will provide you with meaningful information.

As you take the hand of your higher self, you begin to feel yourself floating back through time, returning to a past life that is important for you to remember and become aware of. Feel your awareness slowly and easily traveling back through time, feeling the energies of time as they surround and envelop you. Let yourself fully experience the vibrations of time as you travel through them.

Gently drifting back through time, you begin to see images of past life pictures and scenes of past life events. You begin to become aware of feelings, feelings that belonged to you when you were someone else. As the scene comes clearly into focus, you find yourself in a past life, in an experience or an event that is important for you to be aware of, an event that is significant to your soul. Your higher self is there with you and will explain everything that you're seeing and feeling.

Take a moment to look around you. See if there are any buildings; notice what the landscape looks like; feel what the weather is like. Gather these impressions and let them focus you into where you are right now. As you become centered into this point and place in time in your past life memory, look at your hands to see the color of your skin. How are you dressed? Look at your clothing and touch it; feel its texture. Are you male or female, young or old? Look down at your feet. What type of shoes or foot covering do you have on? As these images, thoughts, and feelings come into your awareness, you become fully involved in the scene you are experiencing as you open up the memories of the lifetime you've found yourself in.

Completely experience the event that you're involved in. If you're alone, notice where you are, what is around you, and what your thoughts and feelings are. If you're with other people, see the people who are there, hear what they're saying, and see what they're doing. You may recognize them as souls you're connected with now. See what you're doing and what is happening. Feel the emotions you've felt before in that situation. Take as much time as you need to completely explore and experience what is happening, to understand why it is happening and how it relates to your present life. Your higher self will provide you with answers and insights, helping you to understand the significance of the event and why you've remembered it.

When you're done with that memory, your higher self guides you into another significant event in that lifetime that may or may not relate to what you've just become aware of and experienced. Again, be fully in the event and experience it. Take your time to completely understand it and to see how what you did and experienced before in that event relates to your present life.

There may be several significant events to see or feel the emotions of in that lifetime, or in other lifetimes, that will help you understand how the events and emotions in your present life came about from those past experiences. Your higher self will guide you to them. When you're in the events, take your time to see them, to let them come clearly into your awareness, to explore them, to learn from them, and to understand how they are relevant to your present life. Let your higher self show you the reasons for everything you're experiencing in your past life, how and why it came about in the past, and to explain how it affects and influences your present life through the energies you've carried over.

Take some time to see what you've done in that lifetime that was important and good. See what you've learned, why you learned it, and how it is special to you. See what you've accomplished and how you've helped both yourself and others. Take some time to enjoy and appreciate all the good that you've created, and to see how the good has carried over into your present life.

If there was anything bad that you've done, or if someone else did something hurtful to you, or if you become aware of a negative situation that happened to you, take the time you need to completely understand the event and your emotions that are attached to it. By doing this, you become aware of how your actions and reactions to the events that occurred in your past lives have caused and created karma. Remember that you can actively participate in the scene, you can be emotionally removed from the scene, or you can be above the scene, watching it happen.

While you're exploring the events in your past lives, ask your higher self for answers and insight. Ask why these events occurred and clearly see your part in them. Talk with your higher self to obtain complete awareness and understanding of the events, and your past and present reactions to them. See how the events, and the emotions that are attached to them, have influenced and affected your present life.

Within your soul, you truly understand the past life events, and all the emotions that are contained within them and connected to them, that you've experienced. You see how your past life experiences and emotions affected you then and how they influence your experiences now. With this spiritual understanding, you intuitively know how to balance the karma in the way that will best resolve the karma. Because you've understood the past life events that your soul has experienced, the reasons for them and your reactions to them, you can choose to do what's right for your soul to best balance the resulting karma.

Perhaps you will choose to balance it while you are involved in the past life event, or you may want to change certain actions and emotions in your present life that you know will simultaneously affect and balance the actions and emotions in the past, or you may want to think about it some more, to gather more information and decide how to best balance your karma at another time. Your higher self is there and will help you to balance your karma, if you choose to do it now. You know what to do to correct and change the energies of the past.

If another person did something bad or hurtful to you, you may want to forgive him/her and then let that person go, blessing him/her and thanking him/her for the experience that helped your soul to grow, to evolve into who you are now. If you've done something wrong to someone else, you can forgive yourself by understanding why you did it, and by knowing how you can make things right. Perhaps forgiving yourself and/or the other person—whichever is appropriate—is all you need to do to balance your karma and begin the healing. Take some time now to balance your karma in the way that is right for you. Take as much time as you need to forgive and bless the experiences.

Now that you've forgiven yourself or others, or balanced your karma in the way that is right for you, you can heal those events or the entire lifetime, and then let them go. You might want to surround the events and the people who participated in them with white light. Or you may want to ask your higher self to show you how and to help you heal this part of your past life in a loving way. Take some time now, as much time as you need, to do a healing.

You immediately feel a wonderful release that the healing brings as you completely let go of the karma that was attached to your soul. By healing the events and the emotions connected with them, you feel the effects of the healing in your body, mind, and spirit. You'll also see the effects of the healing reflected in your present feelings and experiences. But most of all, you feel it in your soul right now.

If you want to or need to, you can move to another event that was significant in that lifetime or in another lifetime. Perhaps it is important for you to be aware of it for an entirely different reason that relates to something else in your present life, or perhaps the next event you become aware of is connected to what you've just experienced. Your higher self will guide you to another significant event you need to see and become aware of, whether it occurred in that past life or in another one.

Again, be fully in the event. See everything that is important to you in that experience; see what occurred and why it happened. Let yourself understand the reasons why you acted and reacted the way that you did. See both the good and the bad in it. Take all the time you need to fully experience it. Feel the emotions connected with that event. See the people who were involved in that event and understand the part they played. You can view as many events and experiences as you need to in any of your past lives. Each one will bring you greater awareness and insight. Take some time now to explore other events that are significant and important for your soul to understand.

When you're done viewing and reexperiencing the important and significant events in that lifetime, and perhaps in other lifetimes, your higher self will guide you to the day of your death in that previous life.

See the events leading up to your death. See how you died. If the death was painful or traumatic, surround yourself with white light to ease the pain that your spirit felt.

See the thoughts you held in your mind, and the feelings you had within your heart. See if there was a dying promise that you made to yourself. Remember what it was, and why you made that vow. If you feel any sadness or anger about your death, explore those feelings. Remember that your higher self is there with you. Remember that you can surround yourself with white light.

Listen as your higher self explains the purpose of that lifetime and how it relates to the purpose you have in this lifetime. See the connections between that past life and your present life. See how the promises you've made to yourself have come into being in your present life. See how the past has affected and influenced your present life, how your past experiences and emotions have caused and created your present experiences and emotions. Spend as much time as you need to gain this understanding and to absorb the information.

When you feel ready, let go of the physical body that housed your soul in that past lifetime. Let go of any feelings of attachment. Take time to experience the release of your soul from that physical form. See your essence rising above the body, your soul going into the ethereal mist in the universe. See if someone is there to meet you, a special soul you knew in that lifetime, or perhaps an angel or another spiritual being who is waiting to guide you into and through the realms of spirit. If one appears to you, take some time to converse with this being, to see what this being says to you and shows you.

You can feel your awareness entering the interim between lives, where your soul exists in its pure form, where you have full knowledge of all the experiences in that lifetime, and in every other lifetime. In this higher frame of spiritual awareness, take some time to reflect on the past *life or lives you've experienced on your past life journey, to completely understand the reasons for the events that occurred, and to see the purpose and meaning of that life or those lives.*

Take some time for your soul to rest in the interim between lives, to rejuvenate your spirit. If the past life or lives you've become aware of were difficult or painful, let your soul rest for a while, to heal itself before it continues on its journey through life.

When you feel ready to continue, explore what your soul experiences in the interim between lives. Travel through levels of light and awareness in your pure spirit form. See what you do in this vibration of energy, what you think about, what you feel, and what life is like in the energy of your soul form.

While you're in this spiritual vibration of pure awareness and knowledge, and you're done exploring because you're becoming ready to reincarnate into your present life, you begin to look at the situations and events you created for yourself to experience in your present life. Look at the pre-birth promises and commitments you made to yourself and to other souls. See the choices and agreements you made that would create the experiences your soul desires to have in this lifetime. See how you're holding true to what you set out for yourself to achieve, or what you need to do to get on course. See what you can do in your present life that will honor what your soul wants to accomplish.

When you are done with this part of your past life journey, and with your travels through the interim between lives, return to your spiritual sanctuary to rest and reflect on everything you've become aware of and to further understand how it affects and influences your present life. Your higher self is there with you. Your higher self is always with you because your higher self is the spiritual part of you. Take some time to talk with your higher self, to ask any questions you may still have or to reach a higher understanding of all that you have experienced. Your higher self will answer any questions you have and will explain everything you've experienced during your past life journey and beyond into the interim between lives that you'd like to understand more completely or have clarified.

Listen to what your higher self says to you. See how the people in your present life were related to you in the past life or lives you've become aware of, and why they are with you now. Ask your higher self to tell you why you were shown your past life memories, what reasons and purposes the past experiences serve in your present life, why you've become aware of them now, and how you can use the knowledge gained from the past to help you in your present life. Your higher self will explain everything you've experienced to give you clear insights into and answers to your past life experiences.

When you are done with your reflections, and you're ready to return to your present reality in this lifetime, you see the rainbow again, the rainbow that shimmered in the sunlight with the harmonious vibrations of the colors that you traveled through as you raised your awareness into your soul.

Reentering the rainbow, you flow softly and easily into the color violet, seeing and remembering all your feelings and past life experiences as you descend gradually and gently through all the colors of the rainbow, flowing into indigo, blue, green, yellow, orange, and red. If you'd like, you can stop for a while in any of the colors to rest in the vibration of the color and what it represents to you.

You feel completely relaxed and comfortable. You're very aware of the spiritual journey you've just taken into your past lives. You've received answers and insights into everything you've experienced, and you've understood how and why your past experiences and emotions have affected and influenced your present experiences. You know that your awareness of past life events and emotions will continue to surface in your daily life and through your dreams.

Take a few deep breaths now as you become aware of your physical body resting comfortably in the chair or on the couch. Take your time to enjoy this peaceful feeling of relaxation, knowing that you've just taken a sacred journey into your soul. Whenever you're ready, open your eyes, being completely in the present here and now, feeling wonderfully relaxed and refreshed, healthy and happy.

⌒ SIDETRACKS . . .
Present Purposes

Your past life journey doesn't end with this chapter; it is an ongoing experience and, in many ways, your spiritual search is just beginning. In the days and months that follow, your past life memories and your understanding of the events and emotions contained within them will continue to surface in your thoughts and feelings, in your dreams and in your meditations, and you'll be more aware of how your current experiences reflect the energies of past life experiences.

You'll become aware of past life experiences that didn't show themselves during your journey, and you'll also become aware of past life experiences that influence your present life experiences through your dreams or flashes of insight, or simply through a knowing sense of awareness or within a meditation. All the understanding and knowledge of your experiences that you've become aware of during your past life journey, and what you become aware of every day, can help you to make your present life better in every way by applying the information and spiritual insights you've gained into all your experiences.

PART V

SOUL
SHIMMERS

———

16

INTERIM BETWEEN LIVES

After death, your soul releases its connection to your physical body. The transition from your physical body into your spiritual body leads you into an energy vibration known as the interim between lives, where your soul exists between earthly incarnations. The death of your physical body is a rebirth into your soul. Crossing over into the plane of spirituality is simply entering into the white light as your soul is reborn into a spiritual body. Within the white light, you exchange your physical energies for spiritual energies. This is the same process that you experience, in reverse, when you are born into a physical body to begin a new earthly incarnation.

In the interim between lives, in this energy sphere of spiritual awareness, you have the complete remembrance and understanding of all your experiences in every lifetime. You know why they occurred and why you chose to experience them. You understand the master plan you have created for all your experiences and the part your soul plays in them through the various experiences you have in all your incarnations. You see the whole picture and how you are evolving your soul.

In this realm of energy and awareness, all your previous earth experiences and the level of spiritual knowing you've acquired dictate your movement forward through these realms of spirit. Parts of these realms are similar to the energies of physical existence, and you may have experiences that are similar to the ones you had on earth, except they occur in a spiritual vibration of energy instead of in a physical vibration of energy. Part of what you experience is directed by your desires, by what you want to experience, in much the same way that you choose your earth experiences because you desire to experience certain things in the manifest world of energy.

There are no set rules as to what you experience in these realms of spirit because your soul, and all that it has experienced in every lifetime, is unique. However, it does seem that there are four phases, or levels of awareness, that you experience in the interim between earthly lives.

The first phase is a time for rest and reflection, where you're letting go of your earth connections from your most recent lifetime. In this phase, you're looking back and evaluating your experiences, you're incorporating and assimilating the lessons learned, or not learned, and seeing how your soul has progressed on its ever-continuing journey of evolvement. You're not so much judging your past experiences as you are simply seeing them for what they are.

You see how well you've done, or not done, in all the experiences and relationships you've had and what your soul desired to achieve with them. You see how you've done in accomplishing what you set out for your soul to achieve as your main purpose. You look at the karma that was balanced or not balanced, and the reasons why. You also look at both the good and bad karma you've incurred in this most recent lifetime. All this information, together with information from other past lives, is what you'll use when you plan your next incarnation and the experiences that you desire to have.

The second phase is a time of discovery, where you're remembering all the knowledge you've earned from all your collective lifetimes, and the karma you've incurred, balanced, and carried over. This information is also put into your subconscious mind for later reference to be used in your pre-birth planning stage. Then you move on as you begin to reexplore your true spiritual nature and the realms of spirituality. This exploration is a time for learning more about your soul and for gaining spiritual wisdom. You completely let go of the physical energies that your soul was associated with as you move higher in these realms.

In the third phase, you're completely immersed in your soul energies. It's a time for spiritual advancement, for learning more about your soul, and for being with other special souls that you've experienced former lives with. At this level, you're free to explore and experience higher levels of spirituality, depending on where your soul is in terms of your evolvement. The experiences you have in this phase are vast and vary enormously, depending on what your soul chooses to experience in this level. In this phase, you may also journey into other dimensions and realities of spirit. Sometimes you visit to experience spiritual learning, for soul reflection, and to further evolve your soul in a spiritual manner.

The fourth phase is a time of direction and planning. You're becoming ready to reincarnate again on a physical plane, and you're deciding what goals to pursue and what lessons to learn. You're looking at the karma that you'll be carrying over into this life and deciding what you want to do about it. You're also deciding what you want your soul to accomplish this time around. You choose your companions and the experiences you'll share with them. You make promises and commitments, both to yourself and with other souls.

This is your pre-birth planning and preparing phase for your present life—the one you're experiencing now in physical form. During this time, you choose and create the energies for the experiences your soul wants and needs to have in your next incarnation to balance karma, to learn lessons, to connect and be with special souls that you love, and to achieve your soul's purpose. You coordinate the timing with other souls that you choose to have certain experiences with, and you set up the situations that will allow you to have the experiences that your soul desires for learning and balancing, to share love, and to pursue your purpose.

As you're deciding what information to bring with you into this lifetime to innately guide you, you pull from the vast resources of spiritual knowledge that you've acquired in every lifetime, and the experiences you've had in the interim between lives—all of which you will put into motion in your new incarnation. You incorporate and imprint this information into your subconscious mind. You always have the ability to remember your spiritual knowledge; you bring your inner knowing—your soul's awareness—with you in your subconscious mind when you reincarnate.

ACCESSING THE AKASHIC RECORDS

During your past life regression, your higher self guided you into the interim between lives, where you saw the reasons for your past life and the purpose of your past experiences and why you chose to have them. You also became aware of choices and decisions you've made about the experiences you set up in your present incarnation so you could balance your karma, learn lessons, be with special souls, and achieve the purpose you've set for your soul to accomplish this time.

Within the realms of spirit in the interim between lives is a storehouse of spiritual knowledge in a dimension of energy where the Akashic records are kept. *Akasha* is a Sanskrit word that refers to an ethereal realm of energy; the records are imprinted within the energies of your soul. The Akashic record of your soul contains every thought, feeling, and experience you've had since the birth of your soul. You have access to this record of your soul's journey, to all the information contained within it, whenever you desire.

You consult your Akashic record after every lifetime to review and record the events of that life. You put all the knowledge you gain in the interim between lives into this huge reference book. You look through it again before you begin each new incarnation to imprint the knowledge within you that you wish to bring with you of the experiences your soul desires to have, and the choices you've made and want to put into effect in this life.

Reading the Akashic record of your soul provides you with everything you want to know about all the lives you've lived in the past, all the experiences your soul has had in every dimension and realm of awareness since the beginning of time, and how they all relate to your soul's journey toward evolvement. The words show you what you created, and why you created it, for your soul to experience.

SIDE TRIP ... BOOK OF KNOWLEDGE

Have you read the book of knowledge that you found inside the rainbow, in the beam of light from the sunshine of the color yellow, yet? The gift of your spiritual knowledge that was offered to you is the Akashic record of your soul's journey through every life you've lived, written and recorded in great detail with descriptive imagery, showing all your experiences throughout the entire existence of your soul in every earth incarnation, and in every dimension and realm of energy that your soul has lived in.

Your book of knowledge is a treasure trove of information about your soul and gives you access to your full spiritual knowing. It's a book that reveals all your spiritual knowledge, a book that shows you the secrets of your soul. In case you haven't had time to read it yet, the following side trip will help you leaf through the pages.

Return to the mountain, to the sunlight in the color yellow inside the rainbow. You see your book of knowledge, waiting for you to open and read. You may want to go into the green garden in the rainbow with your book of knowledge. If you remember, this beautiful, lush green garden was a special place of healing for you and your soul. Or you may wish to bring your book of knowledge, which you found inside the rainbow, into your spiritual sanctuary to read the pages, to look at the pictures to open up your spiritual awareness and reawaken your inner knowing, to read what your soul has written and has always known, and to remember the knowledge you brought with you into this lifetime.

You can read about the experiences you set up for yourself and chose to have so you could evolve your soul. You can see what you've written about creating and following the path that would lead you to your soul's true purpose in this lifetime. You open the book and look at the page the book opens to. As you read the words, they begin to vibrate on the page, then to radiate with a soft glow of light, emanating into rays of energy that form images that swirl into your thoughts and sparkle into pictures in your mind.

The words and their images draw you inside the pages of your book of knowledge as the word-images vibrate and resonate in your mind, moving in rhythm and harmony with the energy of your soul. You touch the picture in the book, the picture in your mind, feeling the texture and energy of the images and the pictures that the words create. When you read the words, they form pictures that come to life—three-dimensional images that vibrate from the pages into your awareness—resonating with an energy source that is inspired by the words and feelings on the pages, by the words and feelings inside your soul.

The book is filled with every experience your soul has ever had. As you look through the pages and read the words that have already been written, your experiences come to life and you completely understand—with a clarity and knowing that goes beyond words—why they happened, why you chose to experience them, and the reasons for them. You feel—with every part of you, with every part of your awareness—the events and emotions inside the pages, inside your experiences, as the words draw detailed and descriptive images and scenes within your mind. The book of knowledge portrays the pictures of your soul, the essence of your spirit, as it speaks to you of the events and emotions in all your lives, and shows you all the various aspects of your experiences in every lifetime.

Read the pages, listen to the words, and watch the pictures of your soul in your Akashic record—your book of knowledge—to see where you've been and what you've done, and to completely understand all your experiences. Read what your soulmates and kindred spirits have written in your book of knowledge through their thoughts and feelings that have imprinted themselves on the pages in your book.

As you already know within your soul, your book of knowledge is also a journal where you can record your thoughts and feelings about the experiences and emotions in your past lives, and the experiences and emotions in your present life as they are in the process of occurring. You can write and rewrite the situations and scenarios in your present life to reflect what you want them to be, to create them within the energy vibrations of cause and effect.

When you're done reading and viewing your book of knowledge, you close it slowly and thoughtfully, knowing that you can open it again at any time to read the Akashic record of your soul. You return the book to its place in the sunshine inside the rainbow within your mind, knowing that you've found a special treasure inside the rainbow.

17

REFLECTIONS
ON YOUR JOURNEY

Remembering what you did and what you experienced in your past lives helps you by showing you why you're experiencing the events and emotions in your present life. This knowledge empowers you to balance your karma and evolve your soul. Remembering your past lives is only one step on your quest for true spiritual knowledge. The end of this book is really another beginning—a rebirth of your soul's awareness. Life is a continuous journey of seeking knowledge through experiences, achieving understanding of those experiences, and evolving your soul into enlightenment.

The nature of reincarnation is beginnings and endings, of journeying through the experiences in your life in a never-ending, always continuing and constantly evolving realm of spiritual growth and knowledge. As you've discovered on your past life journey, you are your own best guide into every part of your life—whether it is your past life or your present life. When you reunited with your higher self, you were reconnecting with your soul and remembering who you really are—a powerful spiritual being.

As this book ends, all the information you've become aware of about your soul during your past life journey opens up new beginnings for you in your life—new pages and chapters for you to read and write in your Akashic record—and new experiences to explore as you travel through your earth experiences in physical form.

As you journey through life, you are traveling a never-ending, always continuing and constantly evolving spiritual path with steps that lead to enlightenment. Thank you for allowing this book to be a guide into your past lives, to help you remember what you've always known.

PAST LIFE JOURNEY SCRIPT

YOU MAY WISH TO HAVE A TRUSTED FRIEND GUIDE YOU THROUGH your past life memories by reading this past life journey script to you, a friend with whom you can share what you are experiencing so that he/she can guide you through your past life experiences and beyond into the interim between lives.

This can be beneficial for several reasons: A close friend is intuitively in tune with you, and will pick up on subtle emotions that you give during the regression. Your friend also knows you very well, and what you are experiencing in your life. He/she can help you draw the past/present connections. By talking with your friend during your past life journey about what you are experiencing, he/she will be able to direct you in an individual manner, helping you to go deeper within your past life experiences, to further explore them.

If you want to be guided into and through your past lives by someone you know and trust, have your friend read the following script before your regression. Agree on the way you wish to be guided through prompts and questions, and arrange any signals that will help clue your friend in, such as raising your index finger when you are ready to move on to another experience. In this way, your quiet time to explore what you are experiencing is not intruded upon.

If you wish to travel on your own, relying on your own inner wisdom and your higher self, read through the following script to get a good idea of where you're going and how you're going to get there. Then just journey into your past soul memories with your higher self. Or you may wish to record it and listen to your own voice guiding you into and through your past life memories.

Stretch out on a couch or sit in a comfortable chair that completely supports your neck and back. Uncross your legs and let your hands rest at your side. Just breathe naturally and normally as you begin to let your body relax, as you begin to feel your body gently relaxing, as you let your thoughts go and allow your conscious mind to become calm and quiet. Just breathe. Just let yourself relax. Just let your thoughts go. Gently focus your awareness on your breathing. Your breathing will relax you and quiet your conscious mind as you direct your attention inward toward the more aware, knowing part of you, toward your spiritual awareness.

Close your eyes and get into the rhythm of relaxing. Take your time and go slowly, feeling and experiencing every sensation completely in the present moment. Begin to relax your body, and to clear and calm your conscious mind by breathing naturally, by breathing deeply. Just let it happen. Relaxation is a very pleasant feeling of peacefulness, a lovely feeling of harmony, of being in tune with yourself. Take a deep breath in and let it out slowly. Focus your attention and awareness on your breathing for a few minutes. Just breathe. Notice how the simple act of breathing begins to relax you; notice how calm you're beginning to feel.

Listen to the sound of your breathing as you breathe in and out, slowly and naturally. Listen to your breathing as you're feeling your body relax, as you're letting your conscious mind become calm as you center your awareness within yourself. Just breathe. As you're breathing in, imagine that you're inhaling positive, relaxing feelings, allowing a peaceful feeling of relaxation to flow softly into and through you, feeling it circulating through you in a rhythm of harmony and relaxation, a gentle feeling of peacefulness and well-being. As you're breathing out, imagine that you're exhaling negative thoughts and feelings, simply letting go of all your worries in an easy, carefree manner, releasing all your thoughts and feelings from your everyday experiences as you allow your breathing to ease all the tension and tightness from your body.

Breathe in the harmony. Breathe out the mind chatter. Breathe in a feeling of relaxation and well-being. Breathe out all body tensions and unnecessary thoughts that crowd your conscious mind as you turn your attention inward toward your subconscious mind, toward the past life memories that you want to open up and explore.

By first beginning to relax your body with a few deep breaths, you cleanse your lungs and clear your mind. As your conscious mind becomes calm and quiet, and your body becomes more comfortable and relaxed, you tune out the physical world for a time as you tune in to a subtle, more aware, inner level of mind. By directing and focusing your attention and awareness inward, you open up your subconscious mind and enter a meditative, more aware, spiritual frame of mind.

Breathe. Just breathe. Simply feel a gentle flow of relaxation drifting slowly and softly down into and through your entire body. Breathe in positive, relaxing feelings; breathe out negative thoughts and feelings. Breathe in the relaxation. Breathe out the tension. Breathe in the calmness and the quiet. Breathe out the noise and the distractions.

Breathe in the relaxation. Feel it softly and naturally flowing into you and through you, filling you with perfect peace and harmony. Feel all your muscles beginning to relax as they let go of all the tension and tightness in your body.

Feel the peaceful feeling of relaxation flowing through your entire body, feeling every part of your body becoming totally relaxed and comfortable from the top of your head all the way down through the tips of your toes. Breathe in and out, gently, softly, naturally. Feel your mind become calm and quiet. Feel peaceful and centered within yourself. Relaxing your body, opening up your subconscious mind, and focusing your attention and awareness inward is a gentle, flowing process, a soothing rhythm and motion. It's as easy and natural as breathing.

By focusing your attention inward, you begin to see and sense your past life images as you open up your subconscious awareness and enter a meditative, more aware frame of mind. Let your subconscious mind move at its own rate and follow your own pace. Just relax and let your thoughts go. Focus on your breathing as you feel a gentle flow of peaceful relaxation drifting softly into and through your entire body. Breathe. Just breathe. You can interact with and influence your level of relaxation simply through your breathing. Let your breathing relax your body, calm and quiet your conscious mind, and open up your inner awareness. Let your breathing bring you into a peaceful, calm, quiet place within yourself.

Just breathe for a few moments, letting yourself become even more relaxed, letting yourself feel completely calm, quiet, and peaceful. If you'd like, completely stretch out on your couch or move around in your comfortable chair so you feel completely comfortable where you are and your body feels completely relaxed. Breathe some more and get into the rhythm of relaxing. Just focus on your breathing.

Breathe. Just breathe. Notice how the simple act of breathing relaxes you; notice how calm and quiet you're feeling. Let a gentle flow, a soothing, peaceful feeling of relaxation drift slowly and softly down into and through your entire body. Breathe in positive, relaxing feelings; breathe out negative thoughts and feelings. As you're breathing in and out, in harmony with yourself, let this soft, easy, peaceful feeling of relaxation gently and naturally flow all the way through you, calming your conscious mind, replacing body tension with a peaceful feeling of relaxation. Feel all the muscles and cells, nerves and tissues—every part of your body—relaxing from the top of your head all the way down through the tips of your toes.

Feel this calming, soothing, gentle, natural, very peaceful feeling of relaxation flowing deeply down into and through your body, into and through every part of you, beginning at the top of your head. Feel this soothing, peaceful flow of relaxation that is in harmony with your breathing, as a very gentle feeling that flows slowly and softly all the way down into and through you, descending gradually through all the muscles in your forehead and your face, relaxing the muscles around your eyes, your nose, your mouth, and your jaw.

Breathe naturally as you allow your breathing to relax you even more. Let this very peaceful, calming, soothing feeling of relaxation—this gentle rhythm—flow slowly and softly down into and through your neck and your shoulders, gently easing all the tension, letting it just drift away, replacing it with a soft, natural, peaceful feeling of gentle relaxation that flows all the way down into and through your back, vertebra by vertebra, loosening and letting go of all the tension and tightness from the muscles in your back.

As this gentle feeling, this rhythm of relaxation, flows softly and slowly all the way down into and through your chest and abdomen, you'll notice that as your stomach muscles relax, your breathing becomes deeper and slows to a more regular, natural rhythm that is in harmony with your level of relaxation. Listen to your breathing as you breathe in and out. Listen to your breathing as you feel ever so peaceful within yourself.

Now that you're feeling much more relaxed, maybe you'd like to move around a little bit, to readjust your position and get even more comfortable. If you want to, take a moment to gently stretch and then relax even more deeply, now that you've let go of all the tension and tightness from your face and jaw, your neck and shoulders, and from your back, chest, and abdomen. [Pause]

Sinking deeper into the couch or comfortable chair, letting it completely support your body, continue to breathe naturally, feeling this peaceful, gentle, soft, easy rhythm of relaxation flow slowly and naturally down from your shoulders into and through your arms, elbows, wrists, hands, and fingers.

Just breathe, feeling the gentle flow of relaxation circulate softly and rhythmically through your body. You feel so deeply relaxed now. Peaceful. Quiet. Soothed, as the soft, easy feeling of relaxation continues to flow gently down from your stomach and your back into and through your hips, thighs, knees, calves, ankles, feet, and toes.

You're so comfortable now; your body is so completely relaxed. You're feeling perfectly relaxed and peaceful within yourself, in harmony with your subconscious mind, completely in tune with your spiritual awareness. Enjoy your calm, quiet, peaceful feeling of relaxation for a while. Just breathe and be, feeling completely comfortable and perfectly relaxed. Enjoy the pleasant feeling of just being. [Pause]

Now that your physical body is relaxed, and your conscious mind is calm and quiet, you're inside your subconscious mind—you're in a much more aware, meditative frame of mind—a spiritual place of knowing where you can open up your past life memories and explore them.

Before you go into your past life memories, you'll be rising through the seven colors of a rainbow. By rising through the energies of the colors to the top of the rainbow, you'll enter an even more aware frame of mind where you're in touch with and in tune with yourself on an inner, spiritual level.

As you ascend through the colors in the rainbow—beginning at the bottom with red, then rising into orange, yellow, green, blue, indigo, and violet—take your time inside each color to completely enjoy, experience, and absorb the color within your body and your mind. Experience the unique energies and vibrations of each color; feel their rhythm and harmony. Breathe the colors inside you. Be the colors inside you. See, feel, and sense the vibrations of each color as you go inside and through the magical, mystical rainbow in your mind.

As you go inside each color, you might see or sense an image or a scene inside that color. Your mind may show you an image or a feeling that will be beneficial and helpful to you. Perhaps you'll see a scene involving several images that move and change as you become more aware of them, or perhaps you'll focus entirely on the vibrations of each color. Accept what you see and feel. Your subconscious speaks to you in symbols and imagery; it's the language of your mind. By accepting the pictures and feelings that your mind offers you, you're opening up your subconscious mind even more and tuning in to your true spiritual nature. The images you see and the feelings you experience inside each color of the rainbow will be meaningful for you in a very special way. The vibrations of each color you experience will offer you increased awareness.

As you continue to breathe naturally, feeling perfectly relaxed and peaceful, perfectly calm and quiet within yourself, imagine an early morning rainfall. Listen to the sound of the rain as it gently taps on your window. The sound is lulling and soothing, comforting and relaxing. As the soft, steady rhythm of the rain continues, you feel peaceful and quiet within yourself. Just enjoy this feeling for a while. [Pause]

The raindrops begin to patter slowly now as the rain softly comes to an end. Looking outside, through the window, you notice that the sky is beginning to clear and you see the sun beginning to emerge from behind white, misty clouds that are floating leisurely through the sky. Opening up the window, you feel the pleasant warmth of the summer day and decide to go outside to enjoy the warmth and light of the sun.

As you step outside, everything looks bright and beautiful. Breathe in the freshness of the gentle breeze and the wonderful scent of the wet earth. Experience the wonderful, refreshing feeling of a rain shower that has just ended. Looking up at the sky, you notice the most beautiful rainbow you've ever seen. The rainbow has been formed by the early morning rainfall and by the sunshine that filters through the soft, misty clouds. The colors of the rainbow are vibrant and pure, a shimmering spectrum of colors that blend into one another, vibrating perfectly in tune with each other, creating harmony within your mind and soul.

It's the most beautiful rainbow you've ever seen. It surrounds you like a perfect dome that touches the earth and the sky. You feel as if you could reach up and touch the rainbow. You feel as if you could breathe in the colors and be inside them. You feel as if you could rise through the rainbow from beginning to end, and go into the sky and the universe at the top of the rainbow.

As you're admiring the beauty of the rainbow, you sense the harmony of the colors and decide to take a magical trip through the rainbow to experience and absorb the colors within your body and your mind. You want to feel what the colors are really like. You want to be inside the colors and in tune with the colors, understanding the unique energies and vibrations of each color. Somehow you know that all you have to do is just relax into the rainbow and feel yourself flowing upward through the colors.

Feel yourself rising up into the rainbow, floating gently upward, rising into the color red at the bottom of the rainbow. Feel the color all around you. Breathe in the color and feel it inside you; feel it gently moving through your body. Absorb the color within your mind; feel your mind opening up and becoming more aware as you begin to travel the colors of the rainbow. [Pause]

Feel yourself rising up into the color orange in the rainbow. Breathing in the color, you become part of the color and the color becomes part of you. Feel it inside you and all around you. Feel it gently vibrating inside your mind. As you absorb the color within your mind, you experience a wonderful feeling of freedom. You feel as if you're standing on the earth and in the sky at the same time. [Pause]

Feel yourself expanding into the rainbow, rising upward into the color yellow. Breathing in the color, you feel it moving gently within and through your body, within and through your mind. As your mind opens up and becomes more aware, you understand the quality and nature of the rainbow, and you understand the quality and nature of inner truth and knowledge. You feel your inner awareness expanding and increasing as you open up your mind even more. [Pause]

Flowing into the color green, breathing it inside you, you feel its vibrations resonating in harmony within and through your body and your mind. As you experience it within your mind, you become more in touch with your inner feelings. You feel the color with your emotions, and you're aware that the color nourishes your body as well as your mind. You feel refreshed and healthy as your body and mind experience harmony between themselves. [Pause]

Expanding your awareness, rising up into the color blue, softly floating and rising higher inside the rainbow, you feel peaceful and tranquil. Breathing in the color, absorbing it within your body and your mind, you feel as if your thoughts are words, and your words are images that spring into action through your feelings. You feel as if you can say and see your thoughts at the same time, and that they're really one and the same, with no difference between the thought and the word. You have a wonderful knowing and understanding that the sky and the earth are really one and the same, with no difference between the universe and you. [Pause]

As you become aware of this, you rise up into the color indigo inside the rainbow. Breathing in the color of intuitive awareness and spiritual knowing inside you, your mind completely opens up and expands into ever-widening horizons that go far beyond what can be physically seen and touched. You have an understanding and a knowing that goes beyond words and feelings. [Pause]

As you recognize and accept this awareness within yourself, you enter the color violet at the top of the rainbow. Breathing it inside your body and your mind, and feeling it circulate within you, the color inspires feelings of awe and reverence. You realize that you've opened up your mind's awareness, and you're experiencing your true spiritual nature. You've opened up the spiritual knowing inside your soul, and you understand all that is within you. [Pause]

You look above yourself, above the rainbow, and see a shimmering white mist. The light filtering through the mist looks comforting and warm. The mist is a universal white light that is very powerful, pure, and positive in its energy vibration. It sparkles and shimmers with the essence of universal light. The light invites you within and welcomes you; it feels protective and secure, peaceful and spiritual, as you breathe it in and wrap it all around you. You may experience or feel white light as a mist, as a very peaceful, spiritual feeling, as a very bright, clear light, or as a shimmering essence. Whatever way you experience it is the way that is most appropriate for you. [Pause]

See, sense, and feel yourself in the white mist above the rainbow. It feels peaceful, comforting, and warm. Immerse yourself in it completely. As you enter this shimmering white mist, it feels warm and safe and secure, filled with a quiet power that is both reassuring and spiritually nourishing. You sense and remember how special this light is.

Gathering it all around you and breathing it inside you, you become part of the light, absorbing it within your body, your mind, and your soul. Breathing in the white light of the universe, you know that this white light is also the vibration of your soul. You know that you are truly a powerful spiritual being, and you feel at one with the light and with your soul.

Breathe in and bring these peaceful vibrations of powerful, spiritual white light energies inside you so that they are vibrating within you and through you, and all around you. As you draw the pure energies of white light within you, you feel it gently balancing and blending your physical and spiritual energies with universal energy as the light cleanses and purifies your body, mind, and soul, as it brings you into harmony with your spiritual awareness, as it keeps you safe and heals you on all levels.

As you bring white light inside you, as the light permeates deep within you, you realize how powerful white light is—how powerful you are—and you simultaneously realize that this same energy resides in a reservoir deep inside you, welling up and releasing the spiritual power you have within you. You sense and feel and know that the essence of your soul is intricately intertwined and interwoven with the universal vibrations of white light, and that your soul is completely in tune with and vibrates to the same peaceful energies as universal light.

Take a few moments to be in the light, to feel the peaceful vibrations, and to experience and enjoy the harmony of your body, mind, and spirit. Just breathe and be in a natural rhythm and harmony with yourself and white light. You're completely comfortable and relaxed, perfectly peaceful and calm, completely in tune with yourself in a higher level of spiritual awareness and knowing. Breathe white light inside you. Completely surround yourself with it. Feel it flowing and circulating in, through, and all around your body, mind, and soul. [Pause]

White light will always protect you and keep you safe on your past life journeys as you travel into and through events and emotions you experienced in lifetimes now gone by. You can also use white light to heal any negative past life events, pain, or trauma. White light is always with you; it is always available to you.

Continue to breathe it inside you. It feels like a breath of pure, fresh air that revitalizes and replenishes your being on every level of your body, mind, and soul. Feel the warmth that flows through your body like a heartbeat, pulsating in a gentle rhythm of protection and safety that feels natural and comfortable as it rejuvenates you with pure and positive energy, as it relaxes and soothes you.

Feel the energy inside you as it circulates through you and surrounds every muscle, every nerve, every bone, every tissue, every organ, every cell, every part of your physical body. As the warmth of white light flows through you, you feel your body gently vibrating and moving in rhythm and harmony with the pure, peaceful, positive energy. It feels natural, normal, and comfortable; you feel completely safe and peaceful, in harmony with your spiritual vibrations.

As you breathe white light inside you, and you accept and absorb it within your mind, you feel your awareness expanding, rising into the vibration of your soul. Breathe white light inside your soul. As you accept and absorb it within your soul, you know that white light will keep you perfectly safe in body, mind, and spirit; it will protect you in all your experiences on your past life journey.

Feel the peaceful, pure, positive vibrations of energy as you breathe in white light, as you surround yourself with it, as you encircle your body, mind, and soul with the white light of physical, emotional, mental, and spiritual protection. Feel white light flowing into you and circulating gently through every part of you. Breathe in the light as you wrap it all around you like a warm and safe aura of knowledge, awareness, and energy. Feel it surrounding you and flowing through you with positive, peaceful energy and protection. [Pause]

White light is a universal source of energy that is always available to you; it blends with your energy, both within and around you, and keeps you safe on all levels. It's peaceful and powerful at the same time. Feel your increased energy and expanded awareness as you completely encircle yourself with and immerse yourself in white light. Breathe it inside you, feeling it circulate within and through you, wrapping it all around you until you feel absolutely filled and empowered with white light. [Pause]

Within the white light, you become aware of a sacred place that is your spiritual sanctuary. It's calm and peaceful, tranquil and quiet. A spiritual sanctuary is a special place of harmony within your heart, mind, and soul where you feel completely natural, comfortable, safe, peaceful, and perfectly in tune with yourself and in harmony with your spiritual vibrations. Your sanctuary is a spiritual place that already exists within you. It's a sacred space where you're in touch with your soul and in tune with your true spiritual nature.

It's a place that waits for you to remember it and to visit it again. It's a place where your soul can renew and refresh itself, where it can rest and reflect. It's a quiet, tranquil place where you enjoy being peaceful, calm, and happy within yourself. A place where you're truly in touch with yourself, where you're in tune with the quietness, gentleness, and peaceful vibrations of your inner nature. Your soul remembers what and where your sanctuary is.

Your spiritual sanctuary may be a beautiful, serene place in the greenness and natural beauty of nature, or it may be somewhere near the soothing sound of water. It might be a beach, where you listen to the sound of the waves and watch them as they gently ebb and flow. It might be a forest, where you hear the wind gently moving through the leaves in the trees, whispering to you. It might be a wide open expanse of earth, where you view the horizon clearly in all directions. It might be a mountain or a valley. It might be a beautiful lake or a brook with stones you can walk across. It might be a sparkling stream of water or a wonderful waterfall. It might be a garden or a meadow with very beautiful flowers.

It can be a place you've been before or a place you create within your mind. Your sanctuary may be symbolic of a feeling you've had or a place you've been where you really felt like yourself and enjoyed being completely natural. It can represent a mood you've experienced where you truly felt in touch with yourself and in tune with your inner, spiritual nature.

It may be reminiscent of a physical place you've been before or a place that you remember from a spiritual memory. It may be a place where you've lived in the interim between lives, where you've experienced your soul in its natural form, or it may be a spiritual place of being-ness or knowing within a multidimensional realm, an energy vibration of pure spirit. It might be a rainbow or it might be the sun. It might be the sky or a cloud. It might be a sunrise or a sunset. It might be the universe or a star. It might simply be the air that you breathe. Your spiritual sanctuary is wherever and whatever you want it to be.

Take some time now to remember and re-create your spiritual sanctuary. See, imagine, feel, and remember your spiritual sanctuary. Take some time to be there, and to enjoy this very peaceful, sacred place within you. Go inside the images and feelings that your spiritual sanctuary brings forth and inspires within you; be completely there. See and feel and be in your sanctuary, in this sacred place inside your soul. Look all around and explore your sanctuary to see and know all that is there, and to understand why it is there. Spend some time here to enjoy and appreciate your sacred space. Notice how you feel in your spiritual sanctuary, what you do, and what you think about. Tune in to your feelings; tune in to your soul. [Pause]

Notice what your spiritual sanctuary looks like. Pay attention to the visual images you become aware of. These images may be symbolic of some of your deep, inner feelings. They may show you scenes from some of your past lives, or offer you the beginning steps into a past life memory. Take some time now—all the time you need—to see all that there is to see, and to explore all the things you become aware of. Take some time to enjoy being in this spiritual place within you, within your soul. [Pause]

As you travel within the worlds of your inner knowing and awareness through the images you see in your mind, the thoughts you hear in your feelings, and the experiences you encounter on your past life journey, your spiritual sanctuary is your safe haven. You can return here at any time during your journey to rest and reflect, to ponder what you are experiencing, or to just relax for a while in the healing vibrations of your sanctuary. You can come into your spiritual sanctuary for any reason and at any time during your past life journey.

In your spiritual sanctuary, you feel in touch with yourself and in tune with your true spiritual nature. You feel very peaceful and quiet, and you feel a heightened sense of awareness and anticipation building inside you. There is a special atmosphere in your sanctuary that you hadn't noticed before, or perhaps you were aware of it but didn't know quite what it was, or maybe you recognized the spiritual vibrations immediately. You sense a special presence that has come into your spiritual sanctuary and you welcome this awareness that is opening up within you. You know that it is your higher self, the highest aspect of yourself who has come to you. You know that it is your soul, ready to appear to you.

You can perceive your higher self in many ways. Each one of us becomes aware of our higher self in a way that is unique to us. Some people sense their higher self as an energy or a feeling, or as a glowing light or a form of light-energy, while others see their higher self as an image of themselves that is knowledgeable and wise in every respect. Some higher selves appear in a symbolic manner as angels, or wise old men, or ancient philosophers or teachers, and some show themselves as a mother or father figure who is nurturing, caring, and comforting. Some higher selves appear as your best buddy.

Looking around your sanctuary, you see that your higher self is there, waiting for you. You know that your higher self has always been there, waiting for you to recognize and remember him or her, and that your higher self will always be there. As you look at your higher self, you experience an incredible feeling of respect and trust, love and joy, that words cannot describe. The feelings are coming from you and from your higher self at the same time. Take a few moments now to become more aware of your higher self and to enjoy the anticipation of fully remembering all those most special and spiritual parts of yourself. [Pause]

As your higher self begins to walk toward you, you feel the positive, loving, spiritual feelings that emanate from your higher self, and you sense the energy and knowledge that radiates from deep within your higher self, from deep within yourself, deep within your soul. As you move forward to reunite with your higher self, with the spiritual part of you, you experience a wonderful feeling of joy and happiness. As your higher self embraces you, you feel yourself merging into knowledge, awareness, and light. You know you've found the higher aspect of yourself; you've come home to yourself, and you've embraced your soul. In your own way, and in the manner that feels most right for you, become more in tune with your higher self, with your soul. Feel the rapport you have with your higher self that strengthens the bond between you as you more fully open up your spiritual knowledge and awareness. [Pause]

Your higher self knows everything there is to know about your soul, and about all your experiences in every lifetime. It is your inner guide and will lead you, with understanding and insight, into and through all

*your past life experiences. Your higher self is your intuitive and knowl-
edgeable guide who will show you what you most need to see, know, and
experience at this time. Your higher self has your best interests at heart
and will guide you with care into and through your past life memories.*

*Your higher self will guide you through everything that you're
seeing and experiencing. Talk to your higher self. Ask questions. Ask
for clarity. Ask why you're being shown the events that you are seeing
and experiencing. Your higher self will explain everything that is occurring to you, and what you are feeling and why you are feeling it, during
your past life journey to help you perfectly understand what is happening and why it is happening. Your higher self will show you the purpose for it in the past and its relevance to your present life by clearly
explaining how the experience relates to your present life, to give you
greater insight and understanding during your past life journey. If your
higher self is silent for a while, it is because you already know the
answers within and can find the understanding within yourself.*

*While you're here in your spiritual sanctuary, you can ask your
higher self for answers about a present problem that may have its origins
in a past life. [Pause] Your higher self will guide you into the relevant
past life and show you how to reconnect with the past life experience in
order to understand and resolve the problem.*

*Your higher self will explain who the current people in your life
were in past lives and your relationship with them in the past. Your
higher self will show you the karma that was incurred between you and
explain the reasons for being together with them again. Your higher self
will help you understand all the aspects of your karma and guide you
through the balancing and healing process. Your higher self will show
you how to heal any negative past life pain or trauma.*

*Within the white light, you see your higher self standing there,
waiting for you in your spiritual sanctuary, waiting to guide you on
your past life journey. Your higher self tells you that it is time to begin*

your past life journey, that you are ready to explore who you were before and what you've done in lifetimes now gone by. You're ready to travel into and through your past life experiences, and to gain the knowledge of your soul. You know that all you have to do is just let your higher self direct you to the experiences in the past life or lives that are important for you to know about and understand in your present life, the past lives that will provide you with meaningful information.

As you take the hand of your higher self, you begin to feel yourself floating back through time, returning to a past life that is important for you to remember and become aware of. Feel your awareness slowly and easily traveling back through time, feeling the energies of time as they surround and envelop you. Let yourself fully experience the vibrations of time as you travel through them. [Pause]

Gently drifting back through time, you begin to see images of past life pictures and scenes of past life events. You begin to become aware of feelings, feelings that belonged to you when you were someone else. As the scene comes clearly into focus, you find yourself in a past life, in an experience or an event that is important for you to be aware of, an event that is significant to your soul. Your higher self is there with you and will explain everything that you're seeing and feeling.

Take a moment to look around you. See if there are any buildings; notice what the landscape looks like; feel what the weather is like. Gather these impressions and let them focus you into where you are right now. As you become centered into this point and place in time in your past life memory, look at your hands to see the color of your skin. How are you dressed? Look at your clothing and touch it; feel its texture. Are you male or female, young or old? Look down at your feet. What type of shoes or foot covering do you have on? As these images, thoughts, and feelings come into your awareness, you become fully involved in the scene you are experiencing as you open up the memories of the lifetime you've found yourself in. [Pause]

Completely experience the event that you're involved in. If you're alone, notice where you are, what is around you, and what your thoughts and feelings are. If you're with other people, see the people who are there, hear what they're saying, and see what they're doing. You may recognize them as souls you're connected with now. See what you're doing and what is happening. Feel the emotions you've felt before in that situation. Take as much time as you need to completely explore and experience what is happening, to understand why it is happening and how it relates to your present life. Your higher self will provide you with answers and insights, helping you to understand the significance of the event and why you've remembered it. [Pause]

When you're done with that memory, your higher self guides you into another significant event in that lifetime that may or may not relate to what you've just become aware of and experienced. Again, be fully in the event and experience it. Take your time to completely understand it and to see how what you did and experienced before in that event relates to your present life. [Pause]

There may be several significant events to see or feel the emotions of in that lifetime that will help you understand how the events and emotions in your present life came about from those past experiences. Your higher self will guide you to them. When you're in the events, take your time to see them, to let them come clearly into your awareness, to explore them, to learn from them, and to understand how they are relevant to your present life. Let your higher self show you the reasons for everything you're experiencing in your past life, how and why it came about in the past, and to explain how it affects and influences your present life through the energies you've carried over. [Pause]

Take some time to see what you've done in that lifetime that was important and good. See what you've learned, why you learned it, and how it is special to you. See what you've accomplished and how you've helped both yourself and others. Take some time to enjoy and appreciate all the good that you've created, and to see how the good has carried over into your present life. [Pause]

If there was anything bad that you've done, or if someone else did something hurtful to you, or if you become aware of a negative situation that happened to you, take the time you need to completely understand the event and your emotions that are attached to it. By doing this, you become aware of how your actions and reactions to the events that occurred in your past lives have caused and created karma. Remember that you can actively participate in the scene, you can be emotionally removed from the scene, or you can be above the scene, watching it happen. [Pause]

While you're exploring the events in your past lives, ask your higher self for answers and insight. Ask why these events occurred and clearly see your part in them. Talk with your higher self to obtain complete awareness and understanding of the events, and your past and present reactions to them. See how the events, and the emotions that are attached to them, have influenced and affected your present life. [Pause]

Within your soul, you truly understand the past life events you've experienced and all the emotions that are contained within them and connected to them. You see how your past life experiences and emotions affected you then and how they influence your experiences now. With this spiritual understanding, you intuitively know how to balance the karma in the way that will best resolve the karma. Because you've understood the past life events that your soul has experienced, the reasons for them and your reactions to them, you can choose to do what's right for your soul to best balance the resulting karma.

Perhaps you will choose to balance it while you are involved in the past life event, or you may want to change certain actions and emotions in your present life that you know will simultaneously affect and balance the actions and emotions in the past, or you may want to think *about it some more, to gather more information and decide how to best balance your karma at another time. Your higher self is there and will help you to balance your karma, if you choose to do it now. You know what to do to correct and change the energies of the past. [Pause]*

If another person did something bad or hurtful to you, you may want to forgive him/her and then let that person go, blessing him/her and thanking him/her for the experience that helped your soul to grow, to evolve into who you are now. If you've done something wrong to someone else, you can forgive yourself by understanding why you did it, and by knowing how you can make things right. Perhaps forgiving yourself and/or the other person—whichever is appropriate—is all you need to do to balance your karma and begin the healing. Take some time now to balance your karma in the way that is right for you. Take as much time as you need to forgive and bless the experiences. [Pause]

Now that you've forgiven yourself or others, or balanced your karma in the way that is right for you, you can heal those events or the entire lifetime, and then let them go. You might want to surround the events and the people who participated in them with white light. Or you may want to ask your higher self to show you how and to help you heal this part of your past life in a loving way. Take some time now, as much time as you need, to do a healing. [Pause]

You immediately feel a wonderful release that the healing brings as you completely let go of the karma that was attached to your soul. By healing the events and the emotions connected with them, you feel the effects of the healing in your body, mind, and spirit. You'll also see the effects of the healing reflected in your present feelings and experiences. But most of all, you feel it in your soul right now.

If you want to or need to, you can move to another event that was significant in that lifetime or in another lifetime. Perhaps it is important for you to be aware of it for an entirely different reason that relates to something else in your present life, or perhaps the next event you become aware of is connected to what you've just experienced. Your higher self will guide you to another significant event you need to see and become aware of, whether it occurred in that past life or in another one. [Pause]

Again, be fully in the event. See everything that is important to you in that experience; see what occurred and why it happened. Let yourself understand the reasons why you acted and reacted the way that you did. See both the good and the bad in it. Take all the time you need to fully experience it. Feel the emotions connected with that event. See the people who were involved in that event and understand the part they played. [Pause]

You can view as many events and experiences as you need to in any of your past lives. Each one will bring you greater awareness and insight. Take some time now to explore other events that are significant and important for your soul to understand. [Pause]

When you're done viewing and reexperiencing the important and significant events in that lifetime, and perhaps in other lifetimes, your higher self will guide you to the day of your death in that previous life. See the events leading up to your death. See how you died. If the death was painful or traumatic, surround yourself with white light to ease the pain that your spirit felt. [Pause]

See the thoughts you held in your mind, and the feelings you had within your heart. See if there was a dying promise that you made to yourself. Remember what it was, and why you made that vow. If you feel any sadness or anger about your death, explore those feelings. Remember that your higher self is there with you. Remember that you can surround yourself with white light. [Pause]

Listen as your higher self explains the purpose of that lifetime and how it relates to the purpose you have in this lifetime. See the connections between that past life and your present life. See how the promises you've made to yourself have come into being in your present life. See how the past has affected and influenced your present life, how your past experiences and emotions have caused and created your present experiences and emotions. Spend as much time as you need to gain this understanding and to absorb the information. [Pause]

When you feel ready, let go of the physical body that housed your soul in that past lifetime. Let go of any feelings of attachment. Take time to experience the release of your soul from that physical form. See your essence rising above the body, your soul going into the ethereal mist in the universe. See if someone is there to meet you, a special soul you knew in that lifetime, or perhaps an angel or another spiritual being who is waiting to guide you into and through the realms of spirit. If one appears to you, take some time to converse with this being, to see what this being says to you and shows you. [Pause]

You can feel your awareness entering the interim between lives, where your soul exists in its pure form, where you have full knowledge of all the experiences in that lifetime, and in every other lifetime. In this higher frame of spiritual awareness, take some time to reflect on the past life or lives you've experienced on your past life journey, to completely understand the reasons for the events that occurred, and to see the purpose and meaning of that life or those lives. [Pause]

Take some time for your soul to rest in the interim between lives, to rejuvenate your spirit. If the past life or lives you've become aware of were difficult or painful, let your soul rest for a while, to heal itself before it continues on its journey through life. [Pause]

When you feel ready to continue, explore what your soul experiences in the interim between lives. Travel through levels of light and awareness in your pure spirit form. See what you do in this vibration of energy, what you think about, what you feel, and what life is like in the energy of your soul form. [Pause]

While you're in this spiritual vibration of pure awareness and knowledge, and you're done exploring because you're becoming ready to reincarnate into your present life, you begin to look at the situations and events you created for yourself to experience in your present life. Look at the pre-birth promises and commitments you made to yourself and to other souls. See the choices and agreements you made that would create the experiences your soul desires to have in this lifetime. See how you're holding true to what you set out for yourself to achieve, or what you need to do to get on course. See what you can do in your present life that will honor what your soul wants to accomplish. [Pause]

When you are done with this part of your past life journey, and with your travels through the interim between lives, return to your spiritual sanctuary to rest and reflect on everything you've become aware of and to further understand how it affects and influences your present life. Your higher self is there with you. Your higher self is always with you because your higher self is the spiritual part of you. Take some time to talk with your higher self, to ask any questions you may still have or to reach a higher understanding of all that you have experienced. Your higher self will answer any questions and will explain everything you've experienced during your past life journey and beyond into the interim between lives that you'd like to understand more completely or have clarified. [Pause]

Listen to what your higher self says to you. See how the people in your present life were related to you in the past life or lives you've become aware of, and why they are with you now. Ask your higher self to tell you why you were shown your past life memories, what reasons and purposes the past experiences serve in your present life, why you've become aware of them now, and how you can use the knowledge gained from the past to help you in your present life. Your higher self will explain everything you've experienced to give you clear insights into and answers to your past life experiences. [Pause]

When you are done with your reflections, and you're ready to return to your present reality in this lifetime, you see the rainbow again, the rainbow that shimmered in the sunlight with the harmonious vibrations of the colors that you traveled through as you raised your awareness into your soul.

Reentering the rainbow, you flow softly and easily into the color violet, seeing and remembering all your feelings and past life experiences as you descend gradually and gently through all the colors of the rainbow, flowing into indigo, blue, green, yellow, orange, and red. If you'd like, you can stop for a while in any of the colors to rest in the vibration of the color and what it represents to you. [Pause]

You feel completely relaxed and comfortable. You're very aware of the spiritual journey you've just taken into your past lives. You've received answers and insights into everything you've experienced, and you've understood how and why your past experiences and emotions have affected and influenced your present experiences. You know that your awareness of past life events and emotions will continue to surface in your daily life and through your dreams.

Take a few deep breaths now as you become aware of your physical body resting comfortably in the chair or on the couch. Take your time to enjoy this peaceful feeling of relaxation, knowing that you've just taken a sacred journey into your soul. Whenever you're ready, open your eyes, being completely in the present here and now, feeling wonderfully relaxed and refreshed, healthy and happy.

Recommended Reading

Andrews, Ted. *How to Uncover Your Past Lives*. Woodbury: Llewellyn Publications, 1996. Offers various methods for getting in touch with past lives through meditation, self-hypnosis, flower essences, and dowsing.

Cannon, Dolores. *Between Death and Life: Conversations with a Spirit*. Huntsville: Ozark Mountain Publishers, 1993. The information presented in this book was obtained from many past life regressions, conducted by the author, in which her clients experienced their existences between physical incarnations.

———. *Legacy from the Stars*. Huntsville: Ozark Mountain Publishers, 1996. Presents accounts of both past and future lives lived on other planets and in other realms of existence.

Chadwick, Gloria. *Exploring Your Past Lives: A Workbook and Experiential Guide Into and Through Your Past Life Memories*. San Antonio: Mystical Mindscapes, 1987; revised 2008. This is the workbook I used in my reincarnation classes.

———. *Discovering Your Past Lives*. New York: McGraw-Hill, 1988. Offers case studies as well as many avenues to open up and explore the events and emotions in your past lives.

———. *Somewhere Over the Rainbow: A Soul's Journey Home*. San Antonio: Mystical Mindscapes, 1992; revised 2007. Explores one of my past lives that I lived in Egypt as a high priest–turned–philosopher. It offers an in-depth look at parallel lives, and how your higher self/soul is in every part of all your experiences.

————. *Future Lives: Discovering & Understanding Your Destiny*. New York: Sterling Publishing, 2008. Explores the simultaneous time-space concept and offers you many ways to journey into the future to discover what your future lives hold.

Cockell, Jenny. *Across Time and Death: A Mother's Search for her Past Life Children*. New York: Fireside, 1994. Details the author's experiences in finding the souls who were her children in one of her past lives.

————. *Past Lives, Future Lives*. New York: Fireside, 1996. Describes the author's experiences through intuition and hypnosis of events in her future lives.

Cunningham, Janet. *A Tribe Returned*. Crest Park: Deep Forest Press, 1994. Describes the experiences of the author and twenty-five people who all lived at the same time in the same Native American tribe.

Denning, Hazel. *Life without Guilt: Healing through Past-Life Regression*. Woodbury: Llewellyn Publications, 1998. Offers case studies and shows how to release guilt that is carried over from past life events.

Fisher, Joe. *The Case for Reincarnation*. New York: Bantam Books, 1985. Explores various aspects of reincarnation and presents several methods for gaining access to past life memories.

Goldberg, Bruce. *Soul Healing*. Woodbury: Llewellyn Publications, 1997. Explores various ways of healing the soul, whether the trauma occurred in a past life or in the present one.

Holzer, Hans. *Life Beyond: Compelling Evidence for Past Lives and Existence After Death.* Chicago: Contemporary Books, 1994. Offers numerous case studies of what souls have experienced after death and before rebirth.

Linn, Denise. *Past Lives, Present Dreams: How to Use Reincarnation for Personal Growth.* New York: Ballantine Books, 1997. Offers many ways to explore and heal events and emotions in your past lives through dreams and visualization. Also touches upon future lives.

Loe, Gerald. *The "Gift" of Healing.* Maywood: Oakwood Publishing, 1990. Offers many healing methods, including healing past lives. Gerald and I did some work together on past life regression and an account of one of my past lives is included in this book.

McClain, Florence. *A Practical Guide to Past Life Regression.* Woodbury: Llewellyn Publications, 1997. Offers case studies and shows what to look for while doing a past life regression for yourself.

Newton, Michael. *Journey of Souls: Case Studies of Life Between Lives.* Woodbury: Llewellyn Publications, 1994. Offers a journey from death through rebirth and describes what you experience between physical incarnations.

———. *Destiny of Souls: New Case Studies of Life Between Lives.* Woodbury: Llewellyn Publications, 2000. Continues into and through the world of spirit and builds upon the author's previous book.

———. *Life Between Lives: Hypnotherapy for Spiritual Regression.* Woodbury: Llewellyn Publications, 2004. Offers the author's methods for entering the spiritual state of being.

Paulson, Genevieve Lewis, and Stephen J. Paulson. *Reincarnation: Remembering Past Lives.* Woodbury: Llewellyn Publications, 1997. Offers ways to access past life memories through meditation and regression, and how to incorporate the past into the present.

Rieder, Marge. *Mission to Millboro.* Nevada City: Blue Dolphin, 1993. Describes a group reincarnation of souls who were together before.

Roberts, Jane. *The Education of Oversoul 7.* New York: Pocket Books, 1973. This novel explores the oversoul concept within simultaneous time and space. An excellent, entertaining, and enlightening read.

———. *The Further Education of Oversoul Seven.* Englewood Cliffs: Prentice-Hall, 1979. Oversoul Seven's adventures continue through the universal realm of here and now.

———. *Oversoul Seven and the Museum of Time.* Englewood Cliffs: Prentice-Hall, 1984. Oversoul Seven experiences life in a physical body.

These three novels by Jane Roberts are published as *The Oversoul Seven Trilogy* by Amber Allen Publishing, 1995: San Rafael.

Slate, Joe. *Beyond Reincarnation: Experience Your Past Lives & Lives Between Lives.* Woodbury: Llewellyn Publications, 2005. Offers methods for accessing information in past lives and the interim between lives.

Stearn, Jess. *Soul Mates: Perfect Partners Past, Present, and Beyond.* New York: Bantam Books, 1984. Offers case studies of souls who were together in past lives who are now together again in the present.

Steiger, Brad. *You Have Lived Before and You Will Live Again.* Nevada City: Blue Dolphin, 1996. Offers case studies and commentaries on the author's experiences with his past life regression clients.

Wambach, Helen. *Reliving Past Lives.* New York: Harper & Row, 1978. Details the results of the author's clients in group regressions.

Webster, Richard. *Practical Guide to Past-Life Memories: Twelve Proven Methods.* Woodbury: Llewellyn Publications, 2001. Offers case studies and includes ways to access your past life memories through methods such as scrying, dowsing, dreaming, and imagination.

———. *Soul Mates: Understanding Relationships Across Time.* Woodbury: Llewellyn Publications, 2004. Delves into past lives and offers case studies as well as ways to find and keep your soul mate.

Weiss, Brian. *Many Lives, Many Masters.* New York: Fireside, 1998. Details the author's reluctant foray into the world of past life therapy in regressing one of his clients.

INDEX